Praise for

INFORM, TRANSFORM, AND OUTPERFORM

"Technology is everywhere. You know that even now you are facing a tsunami out of proportion to what you have ever faced. That's today's wisdom and the real questions. But what about real answers? Not the answers you get from the standard business book that tells you about an opportunity but does not tell you what specifically to do. Well, here's a book that tells you what to do. Think of your life, the tsunami, and other dangers and opportunities facing you. And think of hiring a top-notch group, which can guide you actionably. Then read this book. It's your consultant. Read what the real practitioners are doing, so your theory can have legs, your opportunities can have substance, and you can enjoy a more restful sleep at night contemplating your opportunities, not fearing them."

—Howard Moskowitz, PhD, founding partner,
Mind Genomics Advisors; author, inventor, mentor, and
hero to businesspeople and students alike

"In this time of rapid digital evolution, it's a comfort to have sure-footed professionals like John sharing hard-won lessons from the field and curating seasoned perspectives."

—Brice Dunwoodie, founder,
CMSWire.com and the DX Summit.

"*No business can survive today without understanding and leveraging the digitization of everything. The transformation of the economy is not just about smart devices, it's not just about social media, it's not just about powerful search engines, and it's not just about global access to massive databases. And it's not just about technology. The digital age demands that we redefine from the ground up how organizations operate, how people communicate, and how to develop and implement business strategy. John Horodyski and his colleagues are thinking several steps ahead of the rest of us; ignore this essential guidebook to the future at your peril.*"

—James Ware, PhD, meeting design strategist; author,
Making Meetings Matter

"*The talented authors of* Inform, Transform and Outperform *have collaborated to provide the roadmap necessary to challenge current thinking. They proactively identify a course of action capable of transforming business culture to meet the digital and informational challenges of the twenty-first century. Every business executive has had those great "ah-ha" moments, often in the shower: the glimpses of clarity in facing the disruptive changes that greets us everyday at the office. However, in the workplace, the answers become more convoluted and often seem less obvious. This "must-read" emboldens management to embrace the revolution and confidently embark on a course of innovative transformation.*"

—Dr. Kenneth J. Rotondo, President
Mind Genomics Advisors

*"Information fuels our daily lives, personally and profession-
ally. Our world is changing constantly and with ever-increasing speed. What information means, the ways in which it is
manifested, captured, utilized and protected, are in constant
states of flux and evolution. With so much happening, how do
organizations stay ahead of the ever-emerging challenges and
make the most of new opportunities?* Inform, Transform, and
Outperform: Digital Content Strategies to Optimize Your
Business for Growth *is a welcome and much-needed guide.
It provides an informed and insightful survey of the digital
business landscape, offering solutions for working with content
and information and presenting strategies for managing the
here-and-now while safeguarding the future. This is an indis-
pensable volume for professionals and students alike, whether in
the trenches or preparing for a new career."*

—Dr. Sandra Hirsh, professor and director,
School of Information, San Jose State University

INFORM, TRANSFORM, AND OUTPERFORM

INFORM, TRANSFORM, AND OUTPERFORM

DIGITAL CONTENT STRATEGIES TO
OPTIMIZE YOUR BUSINESS FOR GROWTH

JOHN HORODYSKI

Published by Advantage, Charleston, South Carolina.
Member of Advantage Media Group.

ADVANTAGE is a registered trademark and the Advantage colophon is a trademark of Advantage Media Group, Inc.

Printed in the United States of America.

ISBN: 978-1-59932-755-6
LCCN: 2016936758

Book design by Katie Biondo.

This publication is designed to provide accurate and authoritative information in regard to the subject matter covered. It is sold with the understanding that the publisher is not engaged in rendering legal, accounting, or other professional services. If legal advice or other expert assistance is required, the services of a competent professional person should be sought.

TreeNeutral

Advantage Media Group is proud to be a part of the Tree Neutral® program. Tree Neutral offsets the number of trees consumed in the production and printing of this book by taking proactive steps such as planting trees in direct proportion to the number of trees used to print books. To learn more about Tree Neutral, please visit **www.treeneutral.com.** To learn more about Advantage's commitment to being a responsible steward of the environment, please visit **www.advantagefamily.com/green**

Advantage Media Group is a publisher of business, self-improvement, and professional development books and online learning. We help entrepreneurs, business leaders, and professionals share their Stories, Passion, and Knowledge to help others Learn & Grow. Do you have a manuscript or book idea that you would like us to consider for publishing? Please visit **advantagefamily.com** or call **1.866.775.1696.**

TABLE OF CONTENTS

FOREWORD

As a society, and in business, change is accelerating at an ever-increasing rate. Four primary accelerators are currently driving this change:

1. The Internet of Things (IoT)

2. 3D printing

3. Robotics (big and nano)

4. Biotechnology

These four accelerators will create a world in which every thing and every person is digitized through the proliferation of ubiquitous devices both external and internal to the human body. Every person and industry will be impacted. Biology and information will continue to merge in order to facilitate an evolving society. We see this today with our dependence on personal digital devices such as iPhones and Fitbits. As Ray Kurzweil writes in his book, *The Singularity is Near*, biology and machine will continue to merge in order for man and society to progress at ever-increasing speeds. Learning to manage this digital revolution is the foundation for success now and in the future in order to embrace, learn, and innovate within this revolution. Health care, financial services, transportation, energy, media, retail, manufacturing, and food industries will rapidly evolve and transform leaving those who do not behind. A strong digital foundation will enable new paradigm shifts and new business models to form. The inability to achieve these paradigm shifts and business models will dis-intermediate legacy industries.

The future of a prosperous society and business will be dependent on those who innovate.

Why should you care about the process of innovation? Innovation is the connecting of disparate ideas, inventions, concepts, products, and thought that create new economically viable products and services enabling market-based paradigm shifts that benefit society. The digital world has allowed our world to evolve from hierarchical to network models. The advent of network models is the enablement of paradigm shifts by creating new disparate connections with collective intelligence (both digital and analog), historically not achievable. Paradigm shifts create new business models! Therefore, a new and evolved prosperous world and business is ever changing!

I applaud *Inform, Transform, and Outperform: Digital Content Strategies to Optimize Your Business for Growth* for setting the stage to properly begin the digital revolution journey and enabling society and business to evolve and prosper in this new world. In order to succeed, one must get the digital foundation correct.

This digital foundation is the starting point, and today is an inflection point for all. Embrace the revolution—learn, build, innovate, and prosper or wither in this new economy and world. Time is short. The choice is yours.

Inform, Transform, and Outperform.

Rick D. McNabb
Managing Partner
Optimity Advisors
Washington, DC

ACKNOWLEDGMENTS

"Thank you." —Anonymous

The most satisfying part about writing is rewriting. This book has been written by a talented group of professionals, to both inform and transform. I am forever grateful to them for acknowledging the call to action and finding inspiration in transformation.

We came together as a team to achieve the common goal in telling the story on digital transformation and bring organizations to an optimized state to compete effectively in the digital world.

This book was written on planes, trains, desks, and more—truly a team effort with multiple media. Thank you to Amtrak Acela Express, Air Canada, Delta Airlines, Virgin Atlantic, and United Airlines for helping along the way and providing in-flight Wi-Fi when it was most needed. And thanks for late-night sessions with Brian Eno to light the way.

There have been so many folks along the way who have provided guidance, inspiration, and laughter to make this all worthwhile. Thank you to Peter, David, Ken, Selma, Deb, Todd, Jacqui, Martha, Ted, and all my information-science graduate students over the last eight years.

Thank you team NYC with Kaan, Brad, Ken, Holly, Mindy, Chad, Gretchen, Reid, Dan, Veronica, Meredith, Nick, Mike, Kelly, Gabe, the great folks at Momofuku, and the great baristas at La Colombe.

Thank you team LA with Jesse, Cyndie, Max, Rod, Hiliary, Deb, the good baristas at Espresso Profeta, and the great cocktails at the Beverly Hilton pool lounge.

Thank you team DC with Rick, Teri, Robert, Kristina, and the great cocktails at Off the Record, Hay-Adams Hotel.

Thank you team London with Andy, Madi, Jacque, Gareth, Jeremy, Rory, Emily, Tobias, the great baristas at the Department of Coffee and Social Affairs, and the great cocktails at the Rivoli Bar at the Ritz.

Thank you to team Vancouver with Nikki, Ben, Kate, Lola, Charles (Uber), Pauline, Peter, Sherry, Justin, Tracey, Chad, Kelly, Marian, John B. and the great baristas at Bean Around the World.

I hope you all find inspiration in transformation.

John Horodyski
Waikoloa, Hawaii
March 18, 2016

INTRODUCTION

If you always do what you always did, you
will always get what you always got.
Albert Einstein

This book has been written by a talented group of professionals, to both inform and transform. The concepts and proven
solutions presented in these chapters reveal a strategy for digital
transformation including asking questions, informing audiences,
and building a foundation to bring your organization or businesses
to an optimized state required to compete effectively in the digital
world.

The digital twenty-first century has smashed old ways of doing
business. It is not longer possible to "always do what you always
did"; the outcome will not be so positive as in Einstein's era. Technology has completely changed how organizations create, access,
and consume data and content. Digital innovations have also
created new types of intellectual property (IP) being delivered at
ever-increasing speed. Business strategy for the twenty-first century
calls for innovation in which the tried and tested triumvirate of
people, process, and technology operate in unison. The demands
to deliver successful and sustainable business outcomes collide with
simultaneously transitioning business models. The new strategy for
success is based on the structure of customers, data, and content—
where meaning may be established. There are many examples of
organizations that have understood this and leveraged their content
to invent business paradigms. The ability to look at intellectual

1

property and digital assets from myriad perspectives has the power to transform but is a difficult concept to encapsulate and quantify. At Optimity Advisors, we help organizations master this digital strategy, and this book aims to put flesh on the bones of untapped information potential and offers a range of approaches to realize the benefits of an organization's content, data, and relationships.

GETTING STARTED

Embarking on the journey of building a digital foundation requires attention and preparedness. Start asking questions, and never stop. By understanding and defining fundamental goals and identifying information and content used by the organization a foundation can launch intellectual property and new uses for content. Content *requires a foundation for digital strategy*. Creating a holistic solution around information will play an integral role in how the business generates revenue, increases efficiencies, and enhances its ability to meet new and emerging market opportunities.

GETTING ORGANIZED

A wise educator once proclaimed that there is "a place for everything and everything in its place." Today, this statement is not only true but also an absolute necessity in guiding digital strategy. IP and content can be found across platforms and multichannel selling and distribution frameworks. Media and data can easily be lost as it travels, moves, and links to other data and is transcoded. In addition, information is being collected through more and more devices and mechanisms. In recent years, a new vocabulary describing this has emerged, enticing and confounding business. Two terms in particular have caught the recent zeitgeist:

- **The Internet of Everything (IoE):** Bringing together people, process, data, and things to make networked connections more relevant and valuable."[1]

- **The Internet of Things (IoT):** Uniquely identifiable objects and their virtual representations in an Internet-like structure.[2]

Suddenly the definition of *content* is broadened, as a "center of everything" to be identified, accessed, repurposed, and distributed. The practice of managing content will effectively help organizations take operational control of their data and intellectual property in order to deliver a business's growth potential. *Strategy* in a digital world needs to be intentional and grounded in good design that strives to adhere to business requirements and provides an organized solution for those it impacts. By design, strategy should be intentional and purposeful.

The emergence of the Internet of Things and other platforms will produce more information and data across locations, both within and external to an organization. A better understanding of data and repositories will protect the organization from savvy plaintiffs requesting big data in discovery, inadvertent data breaches, and consumers losing trust in businesses ability to protect personal data.

Data will only continue to grow. There has never been a more important time to make data a priority and to have a road map for delivering value from it. New platforms provide great opportunities for communication, engagement, and risk management. Data

---

1 "The Internet of Everything," Cisco, http://www.cisco.com/web/about/ac79/innov/IoE.html.
2 "Internet of Things," Wikipedia, http://en.wikipedia.org/wiki/Internet_of_ Things.

sharing and collaboration will play an important part in growth as business rules and policies will govern the ability to collect and analyze internal and external data. More importantly, business rules will govern an organization's ability to generate knowledge and ultimately value. In order to deliver on the promise, data must be delivered consistently, with standard definitions, and organizations must have the ability to reconcile data models from different systems.

PEOPLE:
YEARNING FOR AN EXPERIENCE

If you're happy and you know it . . .

Without question, consumers not only hold high expectations but also create them to serve their needs. It has been said "our happiness depends less on objective conditions and more on our own expectations. Expectations, however, tend to adapt to conditions."[3] But what if expectations are out of sync with what a strategy is capable of accomplishing? Consumer expectations need to be gauged at the beginning of strategic planning to ensure that experiences match user expectations. Undeniably, the consumer experience starts with discipline, work, and pursuit of always-evolving, ever-higher standards. Service-providing websites can be personalized through identification of the market segment.

Enterprise systems in a corporate setting also have customers, though the range of needs presented by business users can vary greatly. In both cases, the customer knows what they want and maintains an expectation that the technology can get it done easily and intuitively. Everyone is used to Google search, auto-fill, and

---

3 Yuval Noah Harari, "Were We Happier in the Stone Age," The Guardian, September 6, 2014, http://www.theguardian.com/books/2014/sep/05/were-we-happier-in-the-stone-age.

easy-to-navigate digital environments, so it is important to antici-pate these expectations in order to increase customer satisfaction. Putting consumers, or end users, at the center has been standard commercial practice for many decades, but delivering positive consumer experience is an ongoing dialogue that requires nurturing and sometimes renewal.

PROCESS:
KNOW YOUR IP, KNOW YOUR BUSINESS

Information feeds business; CRM data, finance, HR, customer data, and also rich media, like photos, videos, graphics, logos, and marketing collateral can all contribute to growth and innovation. Attention to how this content has been created, captured, and leveraged and returns value is the key value proposition of a busi-ness's digital strategy. This foundation is the secret that can inspire and provide the groundwork for the transformative digital strategy that expands markets and manages complex, consumer-centered supply chains. The strategy is never finished but is a continual process of leveraging the collective intelligence of a network of consumers and providers for rapidly cycling invention. As long as change exists, a strategy will change. Success starts by defining what your customers and business aim to achieve and then creating a strategy that is flexible and well governed.

TECHNOLOGY:
TRUST AND AUTHENTICITY

Technology is great when leveraged to transform data into information and then information into insight that can generate action and meaning. Collective actions build mutual trust among community members, establishing knowledge-sharing opportunities, lowering transaction costs, resolving conflicts, and creating greater coherence. Trust sets expectations for positive future interactions and encourages participation with technology. Communicating the meaning and purpose of why a technology tool is being used will build trust with its audience and impact positive experiences. Trust in technology and the data flowing through its pipes will lead to greater participation that will increase the information's value and utility. Without trust and participation, no system can produce desired results.

Technology is great when it is leveraged to transform data into information and then information into insight that can generate knowledge—something actionable and meaningful. Data provides the bridge where processes and the technology can be optimized. But if the data delivered does not match the user expectations, then the efficiencies of a personalized consumer experience are lost. Technology is a tool capable of being used to achieve a specific goal. The tool's functionality has the capacity to produce satisfaction when used to perform a particular task. Understanding the needs of users and providing those touch points will increase the perception of personalization and improve the overall experience.

The struggle in managing information within the digital world is as complex as the digital workflows underpinning the efforts. This landscape includes the internal ecosystem and the wider geography of partners and third-party entities. Data provides the link allowing processes and technology to be optimized. But if data does not match the user expectations, then personalized consumer experience won't be provided. The complexity of available data is compounded with the increasing rate of production and the diversity of data formats.

In reading the papers in this book, be mindful of the current situation and the challenges faced. More importantly, be mindful of the people, processes, and technologies that may influence transformation. Information, IP, and content are critical to business operations; they need to be managed at all points of a digital life cycle. Trust and certainty that data is accurate and usable is critical. Leveraging meaningful metadata in contextualizing, categorizing, and accounting for data provides the best chance for its return on investment. The digital experience for users will be defined by their ability to identify, discover, and experience an organization's brand just as the organization has intended.

Value is not found—it is made. So make the data meaningful and manage it well. Start with a foundation, embrace the transformation, and discover the value in content.

PART I

Metadata, Taxonomy, and Search

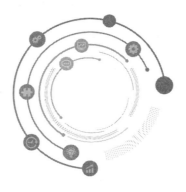

CHAPTER 1

DIGITAL ASSETS AND CONTENT: A FOUNDATION FOR DIGITAL STRATEGY

by John Horodyski

The decision to implement an information management strategy with a content system is a step in the right direction for gaining operational and intellectual control of your digital assets and is to be taken very seriously. Information management brings with it great responsibility for how the organization's assets will be efficiently and effectively managed in its daily operations and is essential to growth. At Optimity, we understand that any successful information management strategy and system requires more than just new technology; it requires a foundation for digital strategy. Creating the whole solution—and connecting it throughout your ecosystem—means that your assets can generate revenue, increase efficiencies, and enhance your ability to meet new and emerging market opportunities.

There are images, video, graphics, 3D models, and more that were either born digital or transformed to digital and that are all competing for attention and use within a multi-distribution-channel framework. We need to take an asset and be able to change it into different formats and then deliver it to television, mobile, print, and social media in very different ways and with various degrees of accompanying metadata. A recent article in Harvard Business Review included the timely argument:

> "Many industries need a long-term, secure way to store their digital assets. Those assets might represent aircraft designs, nuclear power plant operations, oil exploration logs, entertainment content, or government records, but the preservation and access-control requirements are essentially the same."[4]

Managing your digital assets achieves operational control of your organization's information and intellectual property. Manage these assets well, discover their inherit potential, and measure their use for growth—information management may enhance other mission critical systems such as e-commerce and online shopping experiences. The goal is to achieve a single source of truth for all assets within an organization and must be supported by effective metadata, taxonomy, and robust search.

WHAT IS DIGITAL ASSET MANAGEMENT?

Digital asset management (DAM) consists of the management tasks and technological functionality designed to enhance the inventory,

---

4 Rashik Parmar, Ian Mackenzie, David Cohn, and David Gann. "The New Patterns of Innovation: How to Use Data to Drive Growth," Harvard Business Review, Jan–Feb 2014, p. 91.

control, and distribution of digital assets (rich media such as photographs, videos, graphics, logos, marketing collateral) surrounding the ingestion, annotation, cataloguing, storage, retrieval, and distribution of digital assets for use and reuse in marketing or business operations. By definition, a digital asset is any form of content and/or media that has been formatted into a binary source and includes the right to use it. DAM is one of the best examples of an information management strategy in action, transforming the business operations to that next level of optimization.

DAM systems may be developed to house different forms of rich media, including audio, image, and video files along with some amount of descriptive data about the asset. A DAM system aims to improve workflow efficiency through the automation of tasks such as ingest, metadata creation, and authenticated access. In addition, DAM involves not only the stewardship of digital assets—their everyday care and feeding, plus their long-term preservation—but also managing the people and activities that interact with those assets. From IT staff to all users (past and present), keeping a record of what's happened to the assets and how they were used will help plan for their future use. However, there are many things that DAM is not. It is often confused and/or lumped in with other technologies such as web content management (WCM), document management (DM), content management (CM), and records management (RM). The unique and distinguishing aspect of DAM is that it can serve as the single source of truth for rich media assets that demand use and reuse via file format conversions and accessible discovery. DAM is more than a sum total of its parts; it must include a detailed review and analysis of all those contributing factors to DAM: digital assets, organization, workflow, security, etc.

FOUNDATION FOR DIGITAL STRATEGY: BUILDING THE HOUSE OF DAM

Every strategy needs to start with a foundation, that solid base on which some form of structure rests and where meaning may be established. There are many structures to building the "House of DAM" that deserve attention and preparedness for the roadmap of work to be done. More importantly, these are all structures to review and discuss well before any technology has been purchased, let alone considered. *It's commonly known but worth repeating: technology should never lead the decision-making process for DAM demands—the business sets the foundation for strategy first.* Technology is incredibly important, and the vendor review and selection process is a critical step in all this, but that step must follow the business requirements and digital strategy. The following sections outline the major structures of DAM that create the foundation for an effective digital strategy.

FOUNDATION #1—METADATA

Metadata, simply stated, is information that describes other data: data about data. It is the descriptive, administrative, and structural data that define your assets. Besides defining your rich digital media in textual terms, it allows for robust search and the ability for users to find your assets from multiple directions. There are three types of metadata to consider—descriptive, structural, and administrative—that will be further explained in the next chapter. Metadata is the spirit of an intellectual or creative asset, and metadata creation is a strategic imperative for any organization looking to manage and exploit its content more effectively.

FOUNDATION #2—TAXONOMY

Taxonomy is the classification of information into groups or classes that share similar characteristics. The great thing about content is that it frequently organizes itself around hierarchies and order. And, while they are ubiquitous in nature, they are most often poorly understood. Taxonomy is required for meaningful information management and is critical to effective findability, offering consistency and control to language. It is a way to organize information to best solve a business problem based on user needs by exposing relationships between subjects.

FOUNDATION #3—WORKFLOW

The key to good *workflow* is understanding what issues are involved in identifying, capturing, and ingesting assets within a DAM system and then making them accessible and available for retrieval. *DAM may be understood as a workflow device to assist in the marketing operations critical to your organization's needs.* DAM can serve not only as the central source of truth for your assets but also as the infrastructure of the DAM house, the workflow or source of connectivity, on which assets may be moved around from creation, use, and distribution. Now is the time to identify and map out the workflow process of your department and/or organization. In many situations, companies tell the vendor, "Here is our process, automate it," but do not look at the integrity of the process. The search for the right solution should also look ahead to emerging business goals so that the system supports anticipated growth. If the process is flawed and cumbersome, you do not want that to be automated, as the end result will be disastrous. In addition, documenting the workflow is another opportunity to build better relationships with internal teams and partners. The result of this documentation serves as part of the foundation for your DAM solution and the people and processes connected along the way. To determine how a DAM will accommodate your project, it is important to think how and when data is created and modified in your projects, and then think how this data moves through the projects.

FOUNDATION #4—DIGITAL RIGHTS MANAGEMENT

The question to be asked here is, "What can we do with the digital assets we have—from a legal or intellectual property point of view?" *Rights management* provides a company with the ability to track the rights for content it owns, for content it has licensed, and for content it has given to a licensee. There must be serious consideration of any licensing and legal issues associated with your assets, and it demands an understanding of what your assets are and knowledge of how they may be used. No technology alone will solve digital rights management; it's up to the business to ask the right questions. The more that rights management is based on efficient information flow and integration, the faster and more effective the company will be in protecting and monetizing the content it has sold, bought, or licensed. In addition, on the other side of the rights issue is the construction of permissions, users' roles, and security for the DAM that will guide and direct your users to a more successful DAM experience. It is never too early to start working on the business rules and practices around access to content. In one instance, a comprehensive metadata model with fields specific to rights usage and management will be critical for your users' interest in use and reuse.

In another, the application of security protocols in and around your digital assets will protect you for the future.

FOUNDATION #5—DIGITAL PRESERVATION

In regard to archival and preservationist sentiments, the question most often asked is, "Are some of your assets worth preserving beyond the workflow cycles currently under way?" In essence, the question is based on the notion that *digital assets are either for a work in progress (WIP) or for a longer-term notion of storage in a repository.*

This is critical in terms of looking ahead with a view from behind. There may well be sound reason to identify, organize, and centralize your brand assets in a separate location for digital preservation of some kind, whether that is short to mid term, or a much longer-term vision. If indeed a "preservation" problem needs to be solved, then talk to your DAM vendor about this and discern what may be done. In some instances, there are many good examples of using archival assets as a means of procuring new monetization and revenue streams. The discussions around this are made more complex with the ever-growing number of digital assets—and further conundrums such as, "Is my version of this asset as it is used on the iPad a separate asset?" Related to this, the organization's records management and records retention policies are directly impacted by DAM. It is worth the effort to explore new ways of repurposing assets as well as the long-tail usage of assets for potential repurposing in the future. And if the demand is more for a WIP solution, then that too affects the business decisions around the existing workflow solutions. With these answers, you can then identify what functionality the software requires.

FOUNDATION #6—GOVERNANCE

Governance helps us define the *rules of the DAM road*—this provides a framework to ensure that program goals are met both during implementation and for the future. Ultimately, it is the only way to manage and mitigate risk. Governance can begin with a roadmap and measurement tools to ensure success of implementation during the first iteration and may then grow to become formalized into an operating model for the business. These include the regular suspects of a project charter, working committee, and timelines so that governance is an ongoing practice transitioning into an operating model. And beyond the delivery of an effective ROI, active governance delivers innovation and sustained success by building collaborative opportunities and participation from all levels of the organization. The more success you have in getting big names involved in the big decisions, keeping them talking about DAM, and making this a regular, operational discussion (not just for project approval or yearly budget reviews), the greater the benefits from DAM your organization will have. *The best way to plan for future change is to apply an effective layer of governance to your DAM program.* There is more to maintaining the DAM than just maintaining the technology implementation—you must manage the change, and the change is ongoing. DAM is not a project—it is a program. By definition, a project has a finite beginning and end, and a DAM requires considerable attention and governance at all stages and by all stakeholders. In this way, governance is the process, which helps you to ensure that when the initial phases of the DAM initiative are accomplished, you'll have the opportunity to seek further capital and share the next generation of business valuation with executives. Assessing health in governance is one of the most telling indicators and accurate predictors of enterprise DAM success. A best practice in governance is maintaining close alliance with key users and the content steward deployed to operationalize your DAM.

FOUNDATION #7—BUILDING THE BUSINESS CASE FOR DAM

So you think you need a DAM, but why? Now is the time to step back and receive a good perspective of the "who, what, when, and where" of your digital assets and what it is you are trying to achieve. Consider the following examples of what a DAM can do:

- support strategic organizational initiatives

  - reduce costs

  - generate new revenue opportunities

- improve collaboration and streamline creative workflow

- provide better brand management (perception and/or competitiveness)

- enable marketing agility and operational excellence

Brand and market position—and the technologies to support the ever-changing meaning to brand success—are essential to any organizations' growth. The growth curve of demand on the use and purpose of digital assets has outstripped the ability of the internal development team to provide the support required for contemporary enterprise DAM. In order to be successful, leadership will need (and want) to initiate and socialize a process that starts slowly and then works toward a larger end state. Ultimately, this can have direct influence in workflows from packaging to engineering to licensing to social media to focus groups, with full realization of the DAM serving as the key repository, the single source of truth for your assets. Technology adoption can be overly complex and challenging at times, but that does not need to be the case.

In order to harness that potential power, the right people need to be empowered to make change and align DAM with the strategic goals of the organization. Yet, there are still so many questions to ask: Is it a new DAM or a replacement DAM? Is it for marketing operations? Web content? Digital preservation? Is it a singular installation or more expansive for a national audience? There may be many good reasons to implement a DAM system within your organization, not the least of which is identifying, centralizing, and making accessible valuable assets for use and reuse within the organization. And while that is a worthy and most formidable goal to assume, there must be the opportunity to stand back and ensure the problems are being solved with this particular DAM solution.

VENDOR CONSIDERATIONS

It's more than just kicking the tires, it's flipping the car upside down, filling it with gas, running it down the highway, opening it up, and ensuring all the required parts are there from the beginning to the end! *Play before you pay and ensure you have tested it the best that you can.* Vendors expect it. And while you are at it, test-drive two DAMs instead of one, not only to determine which is the best match for you but also to start the often-lengthy licensing negotiation as early as possible. Some capabilities of the DAM to start investigating early are:

- searching and browsing assets

- user interface

- unique IDs for tracking and monitoring

- metadata management and cataloging

- digital asset processing—ingestion, asset creation, and processing

- reporting and analytics

- data security

- customization opportunities

- documentation, training, and user groups

- availability of professional integration consultants

The path to success with DAM is known and can be achieved. It means driving strategic decisions organizationally and technically and ultimately working with a vendor on your technical implementation and beyond as you devise more innovative uses for your DAM investment. Our goal in working together is to look forward and define a framework and to build out the capabilities now that will allow your organization to mature over time and achieve success.

CONCLUSION

Content is still the "king," and the ability to strategically set the foundation for the kingdom and take control of your digital assets with DAM is within your reach. The demand for digital assets used for the design, production, and distribution of content is not only quantifiably high but also qualitatively so, due to its necessity and criticality in current business operations. Simply stated, content drives brand. *You need to get your digital house in order, know what your internal business units and external partners need, and understand how you will need to deliver assets today—and tomorrow—across multiple channels and devices.* Creative professionals and all those working in marketing, communications, operations, and others require content be provided as a cost of remaining competitive and delivering what the consumer wants, when and where they want it. The ability to provide assets of high value and quality in a timely basis is no longer a wish; it is the expectation. And yet, the decision itself to go with a DAM system enacts a chain of questions to be carefully considered before proceeding down the path to DAM. Using DAM effectively can deliver knowledge and measurable cost savings, time to market gains, and greater brand voice consistency—valuable and meaningful effects from your digital strategy foundation.

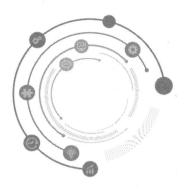

CHAPTER 2

METADATA MATTERS

by John Horodyski

Metadata matters. Metadata is a *strategic* imperative for any organization looking to manage and exploit its knowledge more effectively.

Indeed, these are good times for metadata. It was General David Petraeus's alleged affair that brought metadata into the public spotlight. Thanks to metadata, the Internet protocol addresses pointed to network locations that gave the affair away. No longer was metadata an obscure term reserved for librarians and data scientists modeling content for discovery. It became a notable topic of discussion at the water cooler. And then there was Edward Snowden, whose notoriety from the disclosures regarding the NSA program on collecting metadata on telephone calls is responsible for bringing the term "metadata" to true public discourse, which is more than Melvil Dewey or any other public figure has been able to achieve. However, while it made its way into the modern lexicon, metadata is as misunderstood as it is controversial. Senator Dianne Feinstein argued that "this is just metadata—there is no content involved," responding to the NSA's blanket surveillance of Americans' phone records and Internet activity. But metadata is more than that, and it does matter; there is always content involved, and with that comes value, purpose, and meaning.

The opportunity for content owners, marketing technologists, and all those managing content is in understanding the value that metadata provides their assets and how it can empower their digital operations from creation, to discovery, through distribution.

METADATA IS . . .

Metadata, simply stated, is information that describes other data: data about data. It is the descriptive, administrative, and structural data that define your assets.

1. **Descriptive** metadata describes a resource for purposes such as discovery and identification (i.e., information you would use in a search). It can include elements such as title, creator, author, and keywords.

2. **Structural** metadata indicates how compound objects are put together, for example, how a digital image is configured as provided in EXIF data or how pages are ordered to form chapters (e.g., file format, file dimension, and file length)

3. **Administrative** metadata provides information that helps manage an asset. Two common subsets of administrative data are **rights management** metadata (which deals with intellectual property rights) and **preservation** metadata (which contains information needed to archive and preserve a resource).

And yet, metadata is an "asset" unto itself—and an important one at that. It provides the foundation and structure needed to make your assets more discoverable, accessible, and, therefore, valuable. In other words: Metadata makes them "smart assets." Simply digitizing video, audio, graphic files, and more only scratches the surface of their value as digital assets. Their full potential is realized only by their use, and they can only be used if they can be found. The robustness and relevance of the metadata associated with an asset is what makes it findable and therefore usable.

RELATED METADATA CONCEPTS

Taxonomy is the classification of information into groups or classes that share similar characteristics. It is a way to organize information to best solve a business problem based on user needs by exposing relationships between subjects. A well-designed taxonomy brings business processes into alignment, allowing users to intuitively navigate to the "right" content. The best reason for creating and implementing a single, standard taxonomy across the enterprise is that it provides good business value. But more than that, it enhances and improves enterprise search and enables quick information discovery. Taxonomy provides the consistent and controlled vocabulary that can power the single source of truth as expressed in a DAM or CMS. It is a *key enabler* for organizing any large body of content. It is required for meaningful information management and critical to effective "findability."

A controlled vocabulary is used in drop-down pick lists, and the use of "preferred terms" is a good way to provide authority and consistency to your digital assets. Each tag could point to a different topic, but fundamentally it's the same principal element of the subject under review that is relevant. If the topic is "country" and you only have eight countries with which you work, then those eight countries comprise your controlled list. Control and, stronger yet, authority, is needed to describe your assets. *You need to know what it is you are describing and how it may best be described.*

Structured data refers to information with a good level of control and organization—for example, a "date" value in an "expiration date" field. Structured data is usually found in a controlled data environment with inherent meaning and purpose. **Unstructured data** lacks that control and meaning; it offers a confused sense of purpose and requires analysis or interpretation to restore meaning. Using the example above, if a "date" is discovered with no "field" in which to provide that control and structure, what does that tell you? The interest is in wrangling all that data to create a more structured sense of purpose for the content in your organization; it makes information more relevant, palpable, understandable, and useable.

Master data management (MDM) is the technical discipline/method of enabling an enterprise (both the business and IT) to link all of its critical data to one file, most often referred to as a "master" file for centralized governance.

- **Master data** is business critical data that is governed and shared across multiple systems, applications, or departments within an organization. Master data can be identifiers, attributes, relationships, reference data, and yes, metadata!

- **Master data management** is the set of processes, tools, and governance standards/policies that consistently define, manage, and distribute master data. This could be expanded to discuss the various implementation details.

You can't have MDM without good metadata. Everything starts with data modeling, and data modeling is inherently tied to metadata (ISO-IEC 11179).

Regarding standards, never miss the opportunity to learn more about some of the available metadata standards specific to your industry or application. A **standard** is an agreed level of quality, created by industry leaders and used as a measure or norm in comparative evaluations. Standards need to be evaluated on a regular basis through the ongoing work of the metadata manager/taxonomist. Use an industry standard (or standards) that applies, and then extend it as needed. Consider participating in the standards community by publishing your updates with the governing body.

LANGUAGE IS ALWAYS CHANGING

Research shows that workers waste more than 40 percent of their time searching for existing assets and recreating them when they are not found.[5] This lost productivity and redundancy from the nondiscovery of assets is expensive. The key to avoiding these unnecessary costs is good metadata to aid in search and retrieval and workflow. It

---

5 "The high cost of not finding information," Susan Feldman, KMWorld, March 1, 2004, http://www.kmworld.com/Articles/Editorial/Features/The-high-cost-of-not-finding-information-9534.aspx.

is estimated that, every year, eight hundred neologisms (new words and phrases) are added to the English language, showing how little of our modern language is written in stone; instead, it is always evolving. It is critical to understand that metadata is a snapshot representing the business processes and goals at a particular time. In an ever-changing business environment, metadata must be adaptable and must evolve over time to stay relevant to the digital assets that they support. If maintained and governed well, then metadata can be a very real contribution to your business goals.

The best way to plan for future change is to apply an effective layer of governance to your metadata. There is more to maintaining the metadata than just maintaining the taxonomy and metadata specifications—*you must manage the change*. Vocabularies must change over time to stay relevant, and processes must be created to manage this change. This is also true for new terminology being added to assets as well as synonyms and/or slang terms and more.

As an example, the following images are both "tablets" and so are similar by name but so very different in meaning, depending on the subject and time at hand.

They are all by definition "tablets," but each of them is unique in meaning and value to the user. You need to know what it is you are describing and how it may best be described. If more than 40 percent of workers' time is wasted searching for existing assets and recreating them when they aren't found, then it behooves you to invest the time to get to know your assets, your access, and your users and create an environment that provides meaningful results. The key is good metadata! Your data wants to be found! Develop an incremental, extensible process that identifies and enables users and engages stakeholders with feedback loops, user testing, and evaluations for your metadata. Remember that metadata is a "snapshot" in time. *Take the time to manage your language, and control the change.*

KEY FINDINGS ACROSS INDUSTRIES AND CLIENTS

Our company, Optimity Advisors has been working with clients across many industries, including media and entertainment, health, insurance, consumer packaged goods (CPG), and pharmaceuticals, to help them with digital strategy and information management. Over time, we have discovered common themes among metadata and digital problems:

- little or no metadata planning for new process or systems

- no clear ownership over digital assets and their management

- no current documentation on metadata / controlled vocabulary

- lack of documentation and control over assets

- poor labeling of folders and assets

- agencies, such as external advertising or digital agencies, that are often the default single source of truth

Metadata matters and needs to be addressed at the beginning of any content strategy and not at the end of the business-requirements-gathering process. It is worthy of concern for any practice looking to manage digital assets effectively within an organization.

A NECESSARY DEFENSE

Metadata is the best way to protect yourself and to defend your digital assets from information anxiety and mismanagement. If a good offense is your best defense with metadata as with anything else, then it is worthwhile to invest the time, energy, and resources to identify, define, and organize your assets for discovery. Metadata serves asset discovery by:

- allowing assets to be found by relevant criteria,

- identifying assets,

- bringing similar assets together,

- distinguishing dissimilar assets, and

- giving location information.

Metadata matters and is your best chance for a return on investment on the assets you have created and also a line of defense against lost opportunities. Think about the digital experience for your users and ensuring they identify, discover, and experience your brand the way in which it was intended. It is a necessary defense.

METADATA DESIGN: WHERE TO START?

The path to good metadata design begins with the realization that your digital assets need to be identified, organized, and made available for discovery. The following questions serve as the beginning of that design:

1. **What problems do you need to solve?**

   Ensure that you know the business goals of your organization and how metadata may contribute to those goals. The goal is to be cohesive and not disjointed.

2. **Who is going to use the metadata and for what?**

   Determine who is the audience for the metadata, and consider how much metadata you need; the best strategy is accurate intelligence.

3. **What kinds of metadata are important for those purposes?**

   Metadata may well be expensive; make your model extensible and allow for its natural growth and evolution over time.

Metadata is the foundation for your digital strategy. It is needed to deliver an optimized and fully engaging consumer experience. There are other critical steps to take as well, including building the right team, making the correct business case, and performing effective requirements gathering—but nothing can replace an effective metadata foundation for your digital strategy. As previously stated, you want your assets to be discovered, and they want to be found. Content may still be king, but the user is also worthy because if you have great content and no one can find it, the value of the content is no better than if it did not exist. Metadata will help ensure that you are building the right system for the right users.

CONCLUSION

Metadata matters, and it is neither a trend nor a buzzword. It is a fundamental application of asset management, enabling the creation, discovery, and ultimately distribution and consumption of data and content. Metadata demands attention in effective business solutions. You need to develop and sustain your strategy—from the beginning of the process with the information audit, to the data analysis, and ultimately to the organization of your content for discovery. Stay engaged with your content stewards to ensure that metadata remains current, meaningful, and actionable within the ever-changing digital landscape.

METADATA MATURITY MODEL

Metadata creation is a strategic imperative for any organization looking to manage and exploit its knowledge more effectively. The effective implementation of any content-related strategy—inclusive of data, digital assets, or text—should address overall management by implementing metadata with technology, people, and processes in mind. Applying the Metadata Maturity Model to content management initiatives will provide an agnostic framework for achieving business solutions, introducing a lens through which to understand current use and priorities for discovery, accessibility, and preserva-

tion of content for the future. The five maturity levels are benchmarks that provide an opportunity to discuss metadata development and improvement. Optimity Advisors has successfully used
this framework to help clients expand their strategic offerings and
effectively leverage resources as a key benefit to any information
management strategy.

METADATA MATURITY MODEL		
	BASIC COLLECTIONS	**IDENTIFIED COLLECTIONS**
METADATA ASPECTS:	Entail file-folder hierarchies and pre-assembled collections using file manager of a desktop PC or server; meaning comes from the structure; users infer meaning from project file folder and non-standardized file names.	Represent categorized and tagged group of reusable files, generally finished digital goods or renditions of varying size or resolution; collections resemble "buckets" of potentially useful items with little ability to cull contents into more granular and relevant sets.
Files and Folder Organization	File and/or folder name on a server, shared drive, DVD, etc. May contain suspect data (corrupted, missing fonts or placed art); "right-click" on file reveals basic file properties if any.	Basic level of organization and intelligence behind classification of content for use and potential reuse by identified users.
User Permissions & Access Controls	Self-directed basis.	Create basic file sharing rules including passwords and read/write/delete server access.
Descriptive Keywords	None	Simple functional description such as "brochure" for a brand or market
Search Methods	Scan volumes and file directory of shared disk or DVD (Search PC hard drive)	Simple keyword search, visual scan of thumbnails with basic collections.
Workflows and Projects	Project or brand folder structure in shared drive or CD (Microsoft Project plans).	Basic project stages with simple routing and notifications.
Standards, Policies & Business Rules	Identify and record as needed.	Rudimentary level of standards and practices designed for a basic, useful experience.
Digital Rights	No system in place for rights management.	Simplistic levels of usage rights: "ready for use", "in process," and "classified"
System Integration	None. Much offline in physical media.	Minor linkages with internal systems needed for operations.
Reporting & Usage	No reporting mechanisms.	No reporting mechanisms.
	PROGRESSION SEQUENCE FROM MATURITY PHASE TO 1. Ad Hoc > 2. Organize > 3. Measure > 4. Analyze > 5. Optimiz	

CURATED COLLECTIONS	FACETED COLLECTIONS	SEMANTIC COLLECTIONS
Represent meaningful collections organized for known user types to access; curation emphasizes quality-assured files and task-based use scenarios; most but not all curated collections manage vetted and approved finished goods, but not work in process.	Represent often sizeable groups of diverse sets of files, templates, reusable assets, and business records, optimized for a large, geographically distributed and diverse group of users to access; more than just a collection, this level integrates schedules and release calendars across many project teams, surfacing "coming soon" items.	Enable personalized presentation and user experiences using customer personas and microformats to assemble and bind media and content components into personalized finished digital goods; semantic collections include assets residing in other DAMs, content managers, and social networking platforms.
Embedded EXIF and XMP data and file standards to provide enhanced file description and a richer user experience.	Dynamic presentation of role-based collections, correlating asset profiles and user-engagement criteria; transcends file and folder structures.	Structural metadata for related media components enable access to assets in context of the finished media product.
Identify, create, manage, and enforce rights and roles; regularly communicate these to team and users.	Initial setup of user personas and structured levels of access and control.	Customization and personalized experiences at department, team, and personal levels.
More detailed descriptions of contents, treatments and possible applications.	Detailed descriptive keywords and synonym rings (thesauri) aiding search.	Includes fully developed synonym rings (thesauri) as well as relationships between terms (ontologies) that drive semantic search. Deeply enriched through search analytics practices.
Basic taxonomy in place to serve folder organization and meaningful search.	Rich, meaningful navigation in place in search pages as well as across the system. Search index includes various systems for improved user experience.	Includes meaningful navigation within search pages, incorporating thesauri and ontologies into search experience. Indexes content from across the enterprise.
Full project lifecycle with robust notifications.	Resource scheduling integrated to multiple workflows.	Policy-driven resource allocation and re-tasking across a supply network.
Semi-enforced and structured policies for assets pre- and post-system management.	Enforced standards and rules for departmental and personal use.	Creation of new standards and policies serving personalized workflows and business needs.
Administrative Metadata fields indicating rights, usage and licensing.	Rights metadata refers directly to detailed enterprise policies for rights and asset usage.	Use of DRM tools to serve creative process.
Basic integration with operations systems for approvals and workflow.	Intelligent integration for creative processes and business logic feeding and supporting system.	Increased collaborative tools for self-serving and group work.
Basic reporting in place.	Directed reports tracking the use of assets.	Personalized reporting tools and analytics for power users.

THE NEXT WITHIN a particular type of COLLECTION

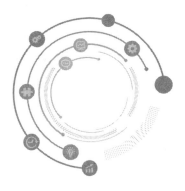

CHAPTER 3

TAXONOMY ESSENTIALS

by Madi Solomon

There are many definitions of taxonomy. The term "taxonomy" is often used synonymously with ontologies, classifications, categories, controlled vocabularies, and even pull-down menus. Whether or not these are truly synonymous (they are not), it only serves to demonstrate the proliferation of dialects that are natural to human beings and should be anticipated in any organization.

When undertaking an information strategy, someone will inevitably suggest the use of a taxonomy to solve the problem of search enhancements, content management, asset findability, analytical insight, auto-classification, rights clearance, and the national security defense for cyber warfare. Before you embark on any taxonomy-as-solution project, there are a few simple rules and definitions that can help focus the effort. Firstly, there is no one taxonomy that will solve all problems. Shocking but true. Conversely, developing a lot of little taxonomies can also be a fool's errand. Regardless of how beautifully tended and nurtured a taxonomy might be, it has no value if it doesn't serve a specific purpose. A taxonomy is never a solution in and of itself.

So what is the purpose of a taxonomy in business? In this chapter, the essentials of taxonomy are explained.

WHAT IS TAXONOMY?

A taxonomy is a list of terms in a classification structure. Although the term "taxonomy" is used rather indiscriminately to describe any sort of classification, a formal taxonomy is typically a hierarchical structure (parent/child) that emphasizes context. It organizes concepts, products, functions, or objects to make them easier to find, identify, and study.

When taxonomies are coupled with metadata, the combination provides a robust content management solution that not only aids in search and retrieval but also enhances navigation and discovery. In any given metadata model, there will be some elements that need to be populated by a controlled vocabulary. The controlled vocabulary is retrieved from the structured taxonomy. Each term inherits intelligence from the taxonomy, which provides context, or domain knowledge. For example, the term *conductor* in a railway taxonomy would be placed differently than one for electrical science.

A taxonomy serves two main purposes:

1. **Harmonize different dialects or expressions.**

   Example: the term *courgette* can be made synonymous with *zucchini* or C. *pepo* in a taxonomy. This tolerance for dialects bypasses the requirement for strict conformity in search queries.

2. **Connect and associate related concepts to each other.**

   Example: The concept of *cooking* can be related to *nutrition* in a taxonomy. If someone did a search on either of these terms, the taxonomy could guide the user to other information tagged with the related term.

Taxonomies can be used to manage assets, processes, objects, and names of things. If applied to marketing assets, for example, a taxonomy could assist in the navigation and "findability" of *modules* such as campaigns, segments, or customer profiles and relate these to the images, graphics, copy, or streaming video relevant to the query.

WHAT IS A CONTROLLED VOCABULARY?

In order to build a viable framework for an asset or content management system, the consistent use of descriptors is crucial if you plan to recommend items or to group things across classifications. A controlled vocabulary, or authority control, is an established list of terms from which a taxonomist, data steward, or metadata manager may select when assigning descriptors to a metadata element within a record representing an asset. This eliminates guesswork, misspellings, and other free associations when indexing digital assets. Consistency in the use of language is only one very important component in sharing and retrieving information.

WHAT IS A METADATA ELEMENT?

Metadata models and schemas are a combination of "elements" or fields of information that help describe a digital asset. *Title, Type,* and *Date Created* are common metadata elements. If you look at your driver's license, you'll see metadata elements that include your height, eye color, address, and so on. While everyone may populate these elements with different *values*, the elements remain standard for everyone. A group of metadata elements is usually called a *schema* or a *metadata model*. An organization may decide to have a Marketing Metadata Model or an Information Management Standard, with a static set of metadata elements that serve as the foundation, or the common license, of items or things they'd like to track and manage.

WHAT DOES A TAXONOMY DO?

The structure of the taxonomy describes what exists and how it is known. By evaluating the placement of a term in the hierarchy or classification structure, a logic is inferred of what kind of content the taxonomy supports.

Taxonomies work directly with a metadata schema or data model and function as the structure of its controlled vocabularies. In the schema of the driver's license, the top categories of the controlled vocabularies for hair color might be blonde, brown, black, red, and gray, with more nuanced descriptors below each. The schema must provide sense and meaning in order to assist users in posing a query and to help them understand the information retrieved.

- Taxonomies normalize descriptive terms.

- Taxonomies structure and organize concepts.

- Taxonomies bridge dialects.

- Taxonomies optimize metadata models.

- Taxonomies offer pathways of discovery.

- Taxonomies provide intelligence through context.

WHY DO WE NEED ONE?

Businesses often discover that the information about their holdings is not consistent with other systems within their organization. Records between collections or acquisitions do not share common guidelines or content management standards, which results in a wide variation of how assets are described. This poses a significant challenge to interoperability (and a huge headache for anyone tasked with data cleansing). Interoperability is essential for understanding the relationships and dependencies of information in multiple systems, and every successful business today requires a combination of perspectives to fully understand its customers and how its operations could be better positioned to serve them. If left unaddressed, asset management, customer relation systems, or financial systems end up duplicating efforts with other related repositories and/or constructing ad-hoc solutions that only further compound organizational ineffectiveness.

Taxonomies help configure a common infrastructure by uniting organizations, partners, and clients in their quest to find, track, and exchange information or assets. Common metadata practices and shared vocabularies in a taxonomy can be used to bridge dialects, concepts, and siloed systems

HOW MANY DIFFERENT KINDS OF TAXONOMIES ARE THERE?

Taxonomy, defined loosely, can be represented in various ways depending on the content or knowledge base it is classifying. Some examples of taxonomy structures are:

- authority lists

- synonym rings

- system maps

- hierarchies

- faceted classification

- thesauri

- ontologies

HOW DO YOU BUILD A TAXONOMY?

Building a taxonomy requires three major components. They are:

1. **Metadata model or schema:** A set of data fields for describing content, objects, or assets to aid access and tracking.

2. **Controlled vocabularies**: An established list of terms from which an indexer or cataloguer may select when assigning descriptors to the metadata model or schema.

3. **Application profile/technology integration:** The formal representation of metadata and vocabularies. Many systems only offer tables with pull-down lists as controlled vocabularies. Others can only utilize taxonomy through a third-party application. Each system of record has their limitations, and the taxonomy must be able to either work within those limitations or have the ability to integrate with a tool.

HOW DO YOU BUILD A HIERARCHY?

Taxonomies are typically hierarchical. It is not recommended to go any further than three levels deep, although there will be times when a subject demands it. For most business taxonomies, however, three levels should be sufficient. The impulse to go granular must be resisted, otherwise too much time will be spent on developing the taxonomy rather than using it to further business goals. There is a common misconception that the more granular the taxonomy, the better search relevance. This is not true, but the desire to overachieve is understandable even if it is misguided. Keep your taxonomy simple and easy to use. The most common taxonomy structures are the genus/species or whole/part hierarchies, and the faceted classification.

GENUS/SPECIES HIERARCHY

Taxonomy originally stems from the biological classification of organisms, where a hierarchy from general to particular, or genus/species, is used to manage nomenclature of species and subspecies. This taxonomy structure describes things that are "kinds" of other things. For example, poodles and schnauzers are kinds of dogs. "Dog" is the parent term, and "poodle" and "schnauzer" are the child terms. A search on the term "dog" would return any assets or information tagged with either "poodle" or "schnauzer" without having to individually type them in a search window.

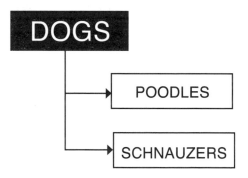

WHOLE/PART HIERARCHY

Another common hierarchical structure for taxonomies is the whole/part approach. This hierarchy describes things that are "parts" of other things. For example, doors, windows, steering wheels, and car seats are all parts of a car. "Car" is the parent term, and the rest are child terms.

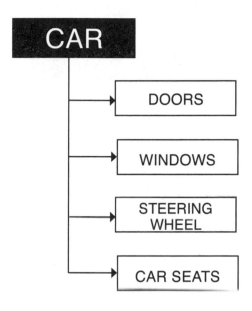

FACETED CLASSIFICATIONS

A broad and flat classification is also a kind of taxonomical structure but not a hierarchical one. Faceted classifications are most often used in business settings where changes regularly occur and the facets, or classification headings, need to quickly respond to growing trends. The Dewey Decimal System is a kind of faceted classification, where assets are grouped by genre like fiction, poetry, and cookbooks. When a new genre needs to be added, like graphic novels, a new facet can be introduced without disrupting the entire taxonomy.

The faceted classification has other advantages over a hierarchy, including polyhierarchy (where one term can be classified under more than one heading), multiple paths to products or assets, the ability to combine terms in order to narrow searches, and easy navigation. Most e-commerce websites use faceted classifications, and users have grown comfortable with this practice.

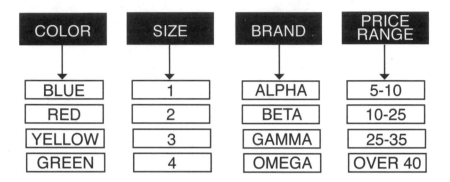

CONCLUSION

Taxonomies in information or asset management can be used to streamline metadata and help cataloguers or data stewards use a common language to describe company assets. Once a common language is established, findability and manageability are increased across systems.

While the essentials as described in this chapter seem easy enough, complexity grows with volume and breadth, and it is recommended to always confirm a taxonomy with a library or information scientist. Taxonomies are living, organic structures and are constantly changing along with the cultures they represent. Remember when gender was described as either male or female? Hair color options have evolved beyond nature's selection to include the neon, ombre, sombre, dip dyed, and tipped. In 2015, five hundred new words were introduced into the *Oxford English Dictionary,* including "FLOTUS" and "Bank of Mom and Dad". Classifications never remain static and true forever. With the right taxonomy, organizations can keep up with the world and their customers.

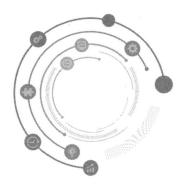

CHAPTER 4

SEMANTIC DATA

by Madi Solomon

In 2014, the World Wide Web celebrated its twenty-fifth anniversary. While it sometimes feels as though we have always exchanged information on the Internet through a myriad of portable screens, we are in actuality the first web generation. The Semantic Web, or Web 3.0, is already ten years old but is still young enough to hold the theoretical promise that our collective intelligence will make information more relevant and pertinent. Evidence is beginning to prove this true as more and more open data is released to the web and data is combined in ways never before possible.

Linked data is a standardized semantic approach to making data inter-relatable so it can group itself with other relevant concepts. By explicitly describing the data in a series of statements, search engines can traverse oceans of data without imposing a prescribed navigation. This approach is particularly powerful with large data sets, but it is not strictly limited to web data. Large global organizations and businesses are also using linked data methods for managing and discovering their own pool of enterprise data.

Standard web protocol language is not a topic of light conversation around the water cooler. This paper attempts to provide a primer for linked data with enough information that should the topic come up, you'll be able to contribute. You may also discover that linked data might be the first step in your big data strategy for integrating information from disparate sources.

WHAT IS LINKED DATA?

Linked data refers to a concept by Tim Berners-Lee, the father of the Internet, for a common practice of exposing, sharing, and connecting information and data on the web. This approach is referred to as the Semantic Web, and it is the next logical evolution from using hyperlinks.

Linked data is predicated on the agreement that everyone will use open semantic standards to participate in a collective "web of data" that can then be harnessed and grouped in intelligent ways. In fact, the more people use it, the smarter the data becomes as more context and information begin to surround the data. Context is where we glean real meaning, so the more information we have clustered or grouped together, the better a computer can make sense of it. The faster a computer can make sense of it, the faster it can parse and deliver it so that we can obtain the information we seek.

BETTA META

How is linked data different from metadata? Linked data is also metadata but better. Metadata helps describe the data; for example, it helps us answer the question "Is the number twelve a grade level, the amount of something, or a floor in a building?" Metadata tells us what the data represents. Linked data works in the same way, but it has the added ability to identify itself and its relationship to other content or data. While metadata is traditionally used in a field table in a database, linked data is mark-up information that travels with the content, asset, or product through an identifier, which eventually creates a graph as it interacts with other data. With this added behavior, linked data is much more than search optimization. It brings intelligence and enrichment to information by being machine-readable so a computer can disambiguate between "Paris," the capital of France, and "Paris," the Hilton heiress, without the use of a taxonomy.

When attempting to integrate multiple data sets, a linked data approach eases the burden by standardizing the data through an intermediary, a kind of metadata layer that can be queried in what is called a triplestore. This is a kind of database that only stores data. They call it a triplestore because the semantic standard used in linked data is expressed in a set of three statements. Because triples in and of itself are a kind of relationship, it is more sophisticated than a simple metadata tag.

EVOLVING STANDARDS AND THE RISE OF THE CONSUMER

In my last job, one of my bosses looked at me askance and said, "No, I don't think so. Standards are firm and don't change. That's why they're called standards!" He couldn't have been more wrong. In the world of technology, nothing stays the same, and that includes standards. Below is a quick timeline of the web protocol standards over the years.

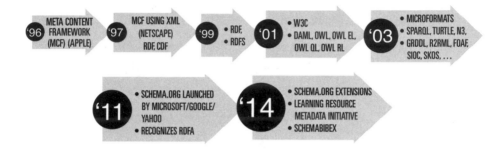

As we've evolved from a "web of documents" to a "web of data," the standards have had to reflect those changes, and each standard was built on the foundation of the standard preceding it.

You may wonder, however, why there appears to be a rather large gap between 2003 and 2011. The simple answer is the rise of e-commerce and the online consumer. Around 2011, developers began using semantic standards to build platforms that were being accessed directly by customers, and this incentivized rapid adoption. The promise of revenue elevated the ideology of the Semantic Web from an academic theory to a practical business imperative.

In the first three years of the release of schema.org 1.0 (a linked data mark-up) in 2011, web pages with semantic extensions increased by 1000 percent, according to Ramanathan V. Guha, the

Google Fellow and founder of schema.org. In fact, Google is already using linked data behind their new search results, though you may not be aware of it.

If you type in the name of an entity in the Google search window—"Tim Berners-Lee" for example—you'll get two sets of results. On the left side of your screen you'll recognize the familiar list of hyperlinks to websites. Regardless of how Google ranks the results, the long authority list still requires human scrolling and reading in order to find the information most pertinent to your inquiry. On the right, you'll notice an information box with links that are specific to Tim Berners-Lee: his birthday, his nationality, his marital status, etc. The information in the box are all semantically linked data and will soon replace the list on the left.

WHAT IT ISN'T

People often misinterpret "semantic" to mean something that has recognizable meaning. They will tell me that they use semantic tags, by way of file headers, or a metadata schema with controlled vocabularies. While these are all good practices, they are not actually semantic. They are not semantic for the simple reason that they are not machine-readable. A search engine may be able to determine the sequence of letters that equal a term, but the term cannot tell the machine or computer what it is, i.e., a grade level, a floor in a tall building, or a currency.

Inserting a URL in a metadata field does not make your data "linked." Using hyperlinks or referencing a website is not semantically linking data. Linked data is the use of standards to express information, so it requires a technical language.

WHAT MAKES LINKED DATA?

Linked data requires the use of open semantic standards such as schema.org, RDF, OWL, SPARQL, and so on.

- It must use URIs (Unique Resource Identifiers) to name things.

- The URIs must also include links to other URIs.

- Linked data is a nonproprietary format.

STATEMENTS IN FORM

Linked data is a method of publishing structured data so that a human, and a machine, can better understand its meaning. RDF, which stands for Resource Description Framework, is the semantic standard for expressing this structured data. It requires data to be expressed as statements in three ways: (1) subject, (2) predicate, (3) object. As mentioned earlier, this is called a "triple." This allows a myriad of combinations to be expressed and shared. For example, we can state the following:

Alice (subject)	has-mother (predicate)	Susan (object)
Alice	has-father	John
Alice	knows	Bob
Bob	has-mother	Martha
Bob	has-father	Dick

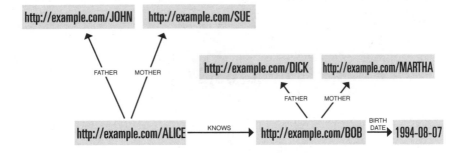

Once every entity becomes "linked," it begins to build relationships with other data, forming a graph, which can be queried, visualized, and analyzed. It's less like a family tree and more like a giant shrub where you can decide to follow Alice's or Bob's relations through a navigational structure that isn't prescribed.

POTENTIAL FOR BUSINESSES

The same theory of integrating and referencing vast amounts of data on the web are equally applicable to most large enterprises. Breaking up siloed repositories and having a holistic view of the data through one interface is a powerful prospect for most businesses. It is more cost effective and efficient than migrating and converging data into one über database, but experience and knowledge in building platforms on semantic technology is still very limited in most IT offices.

Of course, not all data problems can be solved with linked data, and not all databases actually need to reference other databases. It is not a panacea for all enterprise data, but businesses and organizations are beginning to recognize the need to cross-reference and analyze multiple data sets in order to bring evidence into play in decision making. Linked data offers the means of brokering information without disrupting core repositories of content, digital assets, HR data, product portfolios, finance systems, and the like.

CONCLUSION

We are in an age of networked information overtaken by digital components that can be personalized and manipulated by consumers over a vast array of devices. Information management can no longer be dictated by manual efforts. The future of any organization's success is dependent on extending its knowledge beyond content or product distribution to include the listening post placed around it. Tracking and understanding consumer behavior is part of the data evidence that will inform decision. Linked data can be used to build or trigger interventions, recommendations, and outcomes. Linked data may not solve all problems, but data and information are quickly becoming core business assets in and of themselves. Neglect them at your peril.

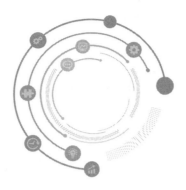

CHAPTER 5

ENTERPRISE SEARCH AND TAXONOMY

by Mindy Carner

When an organization finds that it has amassed thousands of internal documents and assets that are housed in a multitude of different systems, sought by users who consistently look for them in the wrong place, it will often turn to enterprise search as a solution. **Enterprise search** is the practice of collecting content items from within an organization's different systems and indexing them in one place for a unified search experience. However, more often than not, "search" as a practice is misunderstood, with executives wondering why IT can't just "buy one," set it up, and be done with it. This can be very frustrating for information professionals who wish to provide good knowledge management to all that content. Optimity Advisors understands this frustration and has the people and the processes prepared to turn this around and can prepare you for a successful taxonomy for your search. This chapter outlines how enterprise search is not the same as online search and how a taxonomy will fill the gaps between the two for your business operations.

ENTERPRISE SEARCH AND TAXONOMY

Taxonomy is the classification of information into groups or classes that share similar characteristics. A well-designed taxonomy provides the consistent and **controlled vocabulary** that is required for meaningful information management and is critical to effective findability. To use e-commerce as an example of effective use of taxonomy to drive search, Amazon.com is well regarded for its use of taxonomy to help searchers navigate an immense store of content. Whether using the taxonomy to suggest searches in the search box, or using it as the left-hand navigation to browse through content, Amazon. com's navigational taxonomy is a stellar example of how taxonomy is used to improve the search experience. It also showcases how controlling the vocabulary, using the taxonomy, can lead searchers to content that they're looking for.

If you are reading this paper, you are likely wondering about taxonomy for an enterprise search initiative. To work toward the success of an enterprise search project, you should have a trained, dedicated enterprise search project staff in place. This team must include information professionals with library and indexing experience who are familiar with the enterprise search and taxonomy development process. They will provide insight into the size of the vocabulary that will provide the best results, the kinds of terms that will get searchers to the content that they need, and the best way to implement the vocabulary into the enterprise search system.

ENTERPRISE SEARCH VS. ONLINE SEARCH

Without diving into the actual steps of building a taxonomy, the next thing to explain is the set of reasons why enterprise search appliances frequently provide a search experience very dissimilar to what people experience online. The reason that you need to build a taxonomy for your enterprise search engine is that users today expect something similar to their regular online search engine experience no matter where the search box is located. When people perform a search on Google, Bing, or Yahoo, they can expect a large set of results for their query, of which the top three to ten results will satisfy their need. This is because a search engine that indexes the entire Internet's content has different vocabularies, algorithms, and ways of judging "good content" than a search appliance that indexes only a few hundred thousand of your company's assets. This is important to keep in mind because it clarifies why an out-of-the-box search appliance will not, without taxonomy to guide it, provide an effective enterprise search experience for your users.

So what are the differences between an online search engine and an enterprise search appliance? To begin with, indexing the entire World Wide Web requires judgments that do not need to be made in enterprise search. For one, many search engines use **inbound links** to judge a site's credibility. Inbound links are links from other sites to a website. If a website has many links to it, especially from credible websites, then it will get a higher ranking than a website that doesn't have inbound links. This is a very effective way to judge the credibility of a website because it is crowdsourced. However, this does not apply to enterprise search; links to other pages within an intranet does not say anything about the page's credibility.

Another aspect of indexing the web that doesn't play as well in the document repositories and internal content indexed by an enterprise is **sitemap indexing**. A solid sitemap will help a website get higher rankings by making it easier for bots to crawl the site and know its structure and navigation. Many times an enterprise search engine is put in place precisely because the architecture of the repositories has gotten so out of control that sitemaps are not feasible.

The web is primarily composed of HTML pages, images, and videos. An enterprise's digital assets are more often composed of documents but also include webinars, audio files, and images. Internet search engines use structured metadata from HTML to index content intelligently. They use HTML title tags and header tags to understand which words are titles and headings and make those words more important in judging search results. Your enterprise search engine will use these, too—as much as it can. The problem is that enterprises are full of immense amounts of **unstructured data**. Not to mention the lack of metadata around webinars and images on an intranet, all of those PDFs that were born from MS Word files have no HTML metadata to work with, and thus the search engine has no way of knowing which are the important title words that might give some clue as to what the paper is *about*.

HOW ENTERPRISE TAXONOMY FILLS THE GAPS

The above details explain why no out-of-the-box search appliance will provide the same experience as users are accustomed to online. However, it is the reverse view—the aspects of enterprise search that have unique requirements from indexing the web—that will explain how the taxonomy will provide the pivotal key to unlocking a successful enterprise search experience. Below are just a few examples of how enterprise taxonomy drives enterprise search.

1. One of the key reasons that organizations turn to enterprise search is a deluge of documents with no metadata. Documents come with properties forms, but these properties are almost never filled out. Again, this prevents crawler bots from knowing anything *meaningful* about the document. A taxonomy would allow users to choose from a controlled vocabulary of terms to apply metadata to documents when uploading to different platforms such as SharePoint or your company's web content management system.

2. The vocabularies that come out of the box with an enterprise search appliance are not familiar with the internal jargon of your enterprise. This includes internal acronyms, branding, and preferred terminology. Without knowing the context of certain words in your organization, search appliances can fail to give them the proper weight in results. The taxonomy will ensure that the search appliance recognizes your company's vocabulary as important.

3. A strong controlled vocabulary will help prevent the dreaded "no results" page by linking synonyms and misspellings to the proper terms. These "no results" pages are rife in out-of-the-box search engines and rarely offer a useful "next step" suggestion to users who find themselves seeing this frustrating message. The

taxonomy will help avoid "no results" pages altogether by linking synonyms, misspellings, and even acronyms to the terms that are actually written in the documents.

4. **Faceted search** is often offered as an out-of-the-box option in enterprise search appliances. This left-hand navigation for search is so useful for internal searching because it allows users to narrow their search based on key concepts. However, in order for faceted search to be a useful tool, the facets must be built using a custom taxonomy. This way the enterprise controls what shows up on the left, not an algorithm.

CONCLUSION

Knowing these details will help make the difference between a successful enterprise search experience with *meaningful* results and one without. The paper began by defining business requirements to emphasize that this is the key to knowing how to proceed. Moving on to understanding *why* an out-of-the-box technology solution is not enough for enterprise search and then outlining exactly where taxonomy fills in the gaps of the technology, these requirements are the beginning of your search journey.

CASE STUDY: GLOBAL BIOPHARMACEUTICAL COMPANY

INFORM – PROBLEM STATEMENT: MARKET CHALLENGE

Optimity Advisors was engaged by a global biopharmaceutical company who was renowned in the industry for their commitment to excellence in research and development. Operating in a complex, highly regulated business, it is crucial that the company locates and leverage digital assets efficiently while prioritizing corporate governance and responsibility. The client had a track record of prioritizing integrity in communications and compliance, as evidenced by the investment in a digital asset management (DAM) system to organize, administer, and distribute digital assets. In 2014 a critical initiative was launched to evolve business operations in **content deployment** across all brands. The project sought to improve the speed of locating appropriate assets across geographic markets by redesigning and integrating a scalable metadata model and content taxonomy for the client's DAM system. In addition, the goal was to identify opportunities to maximize the value of existing assets. The Metadata and DAM Strategy Project presented an opportunity to evolve the DAM system from an asset repository to a vital tool in the asset development process. There are inherent complexities in creating metadata and taxonomy for a massive organization that has marketing teams around the world. The client creates a large variety of assets for diverse market segments. One key objective of the initiative was to organize and streamline terminology describing marketing collateral produced by siloed marketing teams. The taxonomy needed to address details about intended uses and specific audiences while consolidating differences between cross-border terminologies. The metadata model's design needed to facilitate intuitive navigation of the taxonomy by system users around the world and incorporate rights and usage information for regulatory compliance.

TRANSFORM – STRATEGY, SOLUTION, AND BENEFITS

The new metadata model and taxonomy for the client's DAM system enabled consistent classification and reliable search for assets, avoided excess costs for repurchasing or recreating existing assets and reduced duplicative asset storage. The evolved metadata model also helped manage complex rights and licensing scenarios for each asset, enabling the client to avoid unnecessary legal risks. It additionally provided faster time to market and lower expenditures for asset production and distribution. Initial key beneficiaries of the new metadata/taxonomy were:

- production and library staff responsible for uploading and tagging content for both internal and contractor resources

- marketing, communications, and other end users leveraging existing content to develop marketing collateral while maintaining brand consistency

- third-party agencies needing secure access to assets for sharing and distribution

- additional marketing and communications staff that leverage DAM-managed content for creative inspiration

- various teams needing to access, develop, and distribute assets for internal purposes like training or clinical trials material

OUTPERFORM

Phase 1 of the Metadata and DAM Strategy Project focused on an analysis of current state metadata and the design of an optimized metadata model. The optimized metadata was to also improve the technology's ROI and increase assets' value.

Phase 2 of the Metadata and DAM Strategy Project focused on the definition of a global taxonomy to help standardize the vocabulary currently used by several thousand employees and hundreds of third parties to increase efficiencies and leverage multiple systems beyond the DAM. The goal of the taxonomy was to align the business by creating a common voice and language, contextualize the enterprise vocabulary, and bring disciplined organization to digital assets and information throughout the enterprise. It was important to identify key stakeholders as the priority pilot group to target when rolling out the taxonomy, to socialize it and build networks of knowledge that would garner widespread support.

Phase 3 of the project focused on the creation of a variety of documents to aid with the rollout of the metadata model and taxonomy. This rollout was scheduled to take place a few months after this material was delivered to the client. The final but equally critical section of this phase included documenting governance recommendations for the metadata model and the taxonomy's management. These documents include detailed definitions of key metadata fields, instructions on how they were to be populated, and definitions of new controlled vocabulary lists addressing rights and licenses.

Designing and integrating a scalable metadata model for the client's digital asset management system was a critical initiative necessary to the evolution of content deployment across all brands. The metadata model will help improve search results, reduce asset-redundancy, lower costs, and enable reuse opportunities for archived assets. The model will enable global stakeholders to leverage assets for innovative marketing and communications while maintaining brand consistency. The optimized metadata model also provided the ability for the client to be well equipped in exploring integrating their data with health-care providers' data. The global taxonomy created a unified language for the organization that will help reduce redundancy and increase the communication efficiency across the organization. Successful implementation of the pair will enhance the usability of valuable information within the organization.

PART II

Information Management

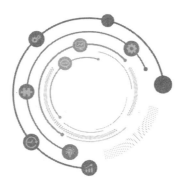

CHAPTER 6

USER EXPERIENCE AND DAM

by Holly Boerner

The question of user experience (UX) in digital asset management (DAM) is one that has bubbled beneath the surface for about as long as DAM has existed. DAM deployments have traditionally sat at a complicated nexus within corporate environments, called on to be applications that provide library-like search and recall of creative assets but also to behave as workflow management systems responsible for facilitating how assets pass through their life-cycle stages. Consequently, end user expectations encountering a DAM have tended to run the full gamut. Users expect DAMs to function as easily and intuitively as Google or Amazon when they're searching for assets they need and also to be as intuitive and easy to use as email or a local hard drive when completing their collection, organization, and file-sharing actions. But embedded within this range of expectations for what a DAM should do sits a singular mandate describing how DAM should feel: easy and intuitive.

The reality is, without providing a good *experience,* users won't want to use a DAM. And as many DAM practitioners can attest, enterprises investing in DAMs with poor UX are setting themselves up for a Sisyphean battle to achieve end user buy-in and system adoption. Failure on that front can be a costly mistake in ROI terms, but poor user adoption will carry additional costs and increased risk for all the objectives DAM aims to achieve:

- operational efficiency

- asset findability and monetization

- asset usage compliance

- analytics-driven insight into asset use and value

Conversely, provide an easy and intuitive user experience and the rest—asset control, metadata management, system usage, and compliance—will follow. *Optimity Advisors understands this imperative and has both the strategic offerings and the resources required to successfully drive holistic DAM UX creation and strategy.*

THE IMPORTANCE OF UX IN DAM

User experience is generally understood to encompass the breadth of elements that collectively influence the experience a person has when navigating technology. UX is most commonly evoked in relation to front-end web development, but it is relevant to any type of technology design—application development, technology products, even general consumer products—really anything a user may employ to complete a task. Providing robust UX has the ability to enable users to perform tasks in such a way that the methodology required to execute an action doesn't hinder but in fact seamlessly, subtly instructs and complements the experience of completing a task. If something is easy, intuitive, and pleasurable to complete, a user will acclimate to performing the action with minimal resistance.

Positive UX can be the decisive element driving a DAM system's end user adoption. If users use the system, it means they will perform digital asset management tasks in compliance with the goals identified by enterprise leadership. Users will do what the business wants them to do, in the way they are supposed to. User adoption means assets will follow desired and optimal workflow paths, they will be enriched by DAM-enabled metadata, and they will be findable and therefore monetizable. At the same time, the enterprise will be protected against legal and monetary risk, as DAM usage will translate to asset usage compliance. System adoption will mean ROI projections are met, and the DAM will be able to demonstrate its potential with a proven track record.

It is no secret that DAM, like all enterprise technology, is increasingly held to standards set by consumer technology. DAM especially faces unique pressure to perform shoulder to shoulder with user experience benchmarks set by technology giants like Google, Adobe, and Apple. It is easy and common for DAM vendors and administrators to try to buy cover in claiming enterprise DAM solutions could never compete with the big three, but as this paper demonstrates, there are many aspects in which DAM can be influenced to achieve positive user experience. It just requires that DAM deployments be approached through the UX lens.

DAM SYSTEM VENDORS AND UX

The good news is that DAM system vendors are aware of this, and as of late, good UX has become a priority goal that many are committed to achieving. For the sake of this paper, many DAM vendors were invited to offer their thoughts about UX and how they are approaching it in product development.[6]

In surveying the vendors, all respondents stressed that UX was an emphatically important priority for product development, typically ranking it as an "eleven" on a ten-point scale. The reasons behind this echoed many of this paper's propositions while including additional motivations:

- Good UX will drive system adoption.

- Customers identified good UX as a desired and priority element in choosing a DAM.

- DAM needs to be as easy to use as email or file-sharing applications (Dropbox, Box, Google Drive) if it's going to be used.

- DAM needs to function harmoniously within larger technology ecosystems.

---

6 Questions provided to vendors were:
    1) On a scale of one to ten, where do user experience (UX) improvements rank on your product development priority list?
    2) Do you distinguish between user experience (UX) and user interface (UI) in product development? If so, what defines the distinction?
    3) If so, on a scale of one to ten, where do UI improvements rank on your product development priority list?
    4) What prompted your prioritization of UX and/or UI improvements in product offerings?
    5) How are you approaching identifying and making UX and/or UI improvements?
    6) How have your customers responded to your product releases where UX and/or UI improvements were emphasized?
    7) What are your near- and long-term goals for evolving and improving UX and/or UI?

- They desire to provide their customers and DAM users an enjoyable experience.

Vendors were asked to describe how they considered the relationship between UX and user interface design (UID), a component of UX often referred to interchangeably as UX. Respondents had different interpretations; some distinguished the two as separate concepts, others didn't—but the contradiction ultimately proved superficial, as the underlying understanding was the same: UID was critical to UX but (when thought of as only the visual component of UX design) not enough on its own to provide robust UX. Vendors understand that user research, persona development, information architecture, and usability concerns also play key roles in determining good UX.

DAM vendors had varying approaches as to how UX was being pursued in product development, but this range seemed mostly to reflect the number of years the vendor has been operating in the DAM market. Those newer to the marketplace expressed a commitment to developing good UX from day one and saw it as an integral part of their product development philosophy. Older, more established vendors explained that they are enthusiastically re-envisioning their systems so that good UX is embedded into their product's core and is not just a superficial UID fix, layered on top of existing functionality.

It is heartening to see vendors prioritizing UX in product development. This is especially important because there are many aspects of UX development that hinge on a system's core engineering. But the reality is that understanding and accomplishing UX in DAM encompasses more than what is provided in an out-of-the-box DAM application; UX is composed of a number of elements that both application developers and DAM administrators and practitioners have the ability—and responsibility—to pursue in order to fully deliver DAM users a positive experience.

USER EXPERIENCE IN DAM

To understand how UX should be pursued by DAM developers and practitioners, its core components of user research, personas, information architecture, usability, and user interface design (UID) should be understood in relation to DAM.

User research—User research in web and application design addresses the goal of understanding who the customer or user is and what their behaviors are in interacting with the application or website. Historically in DAM deployments, enterprises have focused on digital asset management functionality needs, divorced from the environment's real-time digital asset user behaviors. They have prioritized system implementation with key functionality components, without vetting how a user would be tasked to use the identified features. However, DAM is not a system that can afford to be developed without paying equal attention to the people and processes that intersect with its technology in order to achieve success. User research should be performed to identify real-time user behaviors, and the results should be employed as cues for developing the system's behavior and the action mechanisms a DAM should provide.

Personas—On the completion of DAM user research, personas can be defined to delineate the distinct user groups that will interact with the DAM. Considered through a UX lens, the configuration of who makes up what user groups should be defined not just by what they have permission to do or access *but also by what their actual, identified behaviors are in working with assets*:

- Do they perform actions in linear fashion or jump between multiple tasks?

- What gestures do they take to complete a necessary task?

- How many steps are their actions composed of?

- What actions do they intuitively perform without thinking about them?

The key framework to keep in mind in defining DAM user personas is to understand the character, workflow needs, and access boundaries in response to actual identified behaviors, as opposed to being based only on desired or needed behaviors or on what users should or shouldn't have permission to access.

Information Architecture—Information architecture is a technology element that can mean different things in different contexts. In the realm of DAM UX, it is helpful to consider DAM's metadata, controlled vocabulary, and taxonomy components as data points that structure its information architecture. An information classification strategy that facilitates digital asset organization, storage, search, and retrieval is one of the most foundational components of any DAM. But it is important to additionally recognize metadata's value according to a formal UX framework and understand that this fundamental concept in determining asset findability anchors natively within the context of UX. Pursuit of easy asset discovery is deeply dependent on effective information architecture in the form of a smart metadata strategy.

Optimity Advisors has deep experience in providing solid metadata strategies for DAM system implementations and redesigns. Our team understands that not only is navigation and search a fundamental component of the success of a DAM program, but it is also inextricably interlaced with the other aspects of UX—usability, personas, user research, and UID—such that even a solid metadata strategy cannot save a DAM system with poor overall user experience.

Usability—Usability borders on self-explanatory in that it evokes how easy it is for users to use a website or application. In DAM, usability is the framework where features and functionality like search, retrieval, asset distribution, and so on should be considered in relation to UX. Usability starts to encroach on UX territory that DAM administrators generally have limited means to influence, as usability is typically determined by an application's core engineering. It is important that DAM application developers—as the authors capable of determining the behavior and feel of a feature—consider functionality development according to its usability so that features complement and contribute to positive user experience rather than sit divorced from it.

User Interface Design—User interface design (UID) encompasses the holistic design of interfaces. It is composed of both the visual and interactive elements of how a website or application's pages and functionality look and feel. UID should be emphasized in understanding UX, as it is a key component and is often referred to metonymically as UX, but this is a mistake. *User interface design is just one component of user experience.* If user experience is interpreted as only user interface design, opportunities to influence and positively impact UX through user research, personas, information architecture, and usability will be missed.

UID does not require translation or interpretation from how it is understood as an agnostic UX concept when considering it in relation to DAM. Similar to usability, UID is an element that DAM practitioners typically have limited opportunity to influence.

In systems that provide configurable UI components, or in open source applications that allow customers to perform front-end development, system administrators can impact a DAM's user interface design. But the majority of the time, UID sits squarely in the lap of the DAM's application developer to build.

UID in DAM should be held to the same level of accountability it is held to in general website or application development: to be attentive to navigation and to anticipate and complement how users will get around a system while minimizing redundant actions. UID should subtly instruct users along a single, clear path when navigating the system. It is important that UID is developed so that visual and interaction design are deeply intertwined, and the two function as a seamless whole that facilitates ease of navigation and task execution. UID should aim to eliminate any situation in which users experience frustration. Frustration causes users to abandon the system and even find a way to work around it—scenarios many DAM practitioners can likely attest to witnessing.

Finally, perhaps most obvious, good visual design within UID is critical. Users will respond to a beautifully, intuitively designed system with limited functionality much more reliably than to a feature-packed application that is complicated to learn, difficult to use, or ugly to look at.

CONCLUSION

It is encouraging to encounter vendor feedback that affirms UX as a priority in DAM application development, as this reality underscores that UX is a critical element of DAM. As enterprises confront the need to pursue positive and robust UX, Optimity Advisors can provide the holistic guidance and strategy that will build a foundation for a positive user experience by focusing not just on key system features but also on the larger picture of the end user's needs. This will ensure that the DAM can meet its business goals and contribute to the enterprise's ongoing growth and success.

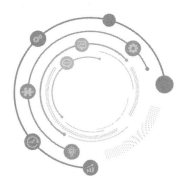

CHAPTER 7

RIGHTS MANAGEMENT

by Chad Beer and Julia Goodwin

Content is proliferating and ubiquitous in this time of digital transformation. We have smartphones, tablets, laptops, all manner of digital devices, and televisions that can act like all of them. Social media makes it easy for everyone to share images, video, and music around the world. We have services and apps that present content based on our individual preferences. There is a lot going on behind the scenes to make this often-flawless digital dance perform for us when we want it and where we want it. The choreographer of this dance is the contract that defines the rights to the content: what can be done with it, by whom, when, where, and how. If content is what we view, the content's rights are what gives a particular person or company the permission to show it to us at that particular time, in a particular way.

Content rights are far more complex than one might imagine. Managing those rights—recording them and keeping them associated with the correct content, and communicating them clearly to those who wish to use that content—is even more challenging. Fortunately, the same factors that create our current complex consumption and distribution environment have also created solutions to nimbly manage rights. Systematized and automated workflows, and detailed metadata and integration between systems, fuel a robust environment and make amazing things possible.

This chapter presents an overview of the intricacies and ramifications of rights management and gives a peek at what can be possible within an optimized digital ecosystem.

RIGHTS, AND RISK, ARE ALL AROUND

What are the content types and use cases that involve rights? All of them. Even a ninth-grader writing her term paper and illustrating it with images downloaded from the Internet is intersecting with rights, whether she knows it or not. It is important that we recognize that the content we see everyday, and the usage of it, involves an intersection of rights and risk. While this ninth-grader is unlikely to be sued, a company using the same images in an e-book, a historical TV documentary, or a marketing campaign can incur real and costly litigation. Any organization producing, selling, or distributing material needs to be very aware of the rights they own for every item of content utilized. A rights violation in such a case may well lead to a lawsuit and a significant financial hit.

A SPECTRUM OF COMPLEXITY

Just as companies, products, and services vary in size and complexity, so it is with content and rights. Some content comes with very simple, straightforward rights. Many royalty-free stock images, for instance, may be used after purchase in any way imaginable, forever. Other content has rights restrictions limiting use based on factors such as geographical location, language, time period, and distribution channel. These rights may also have complex payment structures tied to their use.

There is no one formula defining how all companies should manage rights. Rights should be managed in the way that best allows the workflows of a company to proceed unhindered, with rights information relayed accurately and quickly under disruptive and accelerating conditions. The endgame is for those owning and buying (or licensing) content to be financially successful while anticipating and fulfilling the business opportunities for that content. When rights can flow, content can quickly go.

RIGHTS MANAGEMENT SYSTEMS

Years ago, before software could help, rights management involved a great many filing cabinets and the careful legal analysis of a company's contracts by attorneys in order to determine what a company could do with its content. Today, the capture and communication of rights information and the proper subsequent distribution of that content may be accomplished by a single system specifically designed for that purpose or by many systems integrated along the workflow, from contracting to distribution. There are many good rights management systems available on the market, and very large companies have also developed and coded their own.

Some organizations, particularly those working with less complex rights scenarios, leverage other systems to simplify or partially automate rights management tasks. Contract management systems, content management systems, digital asset management systems, workflow tools, metadata schemas, and the like can all be utilized to help capture and communicate rights information within an organization. Using such systems is often part of a patchwork solution. The systems or solutions used for rights management can depend on the organization's content usage and rights maturity.

To achieve true digital transformation, content-using organizations must consider utilizing a dedicated rights management system (RMS) as part of its operational environment. When integrated with content management systems and by facilitating digital workflows, an RMS ultimately accelerates the ability to pounce on business opportunities while reducing legal risk. We will delve more deeply into what a digitally optimized rights management environment looks like later in this chapter.

DEVELOPING A DIGITIZED RIGHTS MANAGEMENT STRATEGY

In our content-rich world, with assets and delivery channels proliferating exponentially, any organization working with content must decide how to manage rights. Determining the best strategy depends on multiple factors. Let's examine some essential aspects an organization should consider when deciding how it will tackle this challenge. It is important to set the expectation up, early and often, that a digital transformation initiative for rights of any size can be a full-time endeavor for a core project team and will require the dedicated time and buy-in of stakeholders, executives, users, IT partners, vendors, and consultants/experts.

THE INTERNAL RIGHTS, CONTRACTING, AND TRANSACTION LANDSCAPE

What types of content and rights does the organization acquire, sell, or license? How is that content used? A thorough assessment of the various rights and contracting scenarios is an essential activity for transforming the rights management landscape. Does the organization use standardized contracts, and if so, what rights are accommodated? What limitations or exceptions to rights can exist in those contracts? Are content rights sold or licensed out to other organizations? Are there standard contracts and rights scenarios for those exchanges?

Evaluating the financial transactions involving rights is critical when deciding strategic priorities. What rights transactions drive the business? Is significant time and energy put into purchasing rights, while licensing rights to other entities remains uncommon, or is licensing rights to your organization's content a vital source of revenue? Which negotiations are most common or cumbersome to the people involved in managing them? Are they too cumbersome to capture or even enforce? What business opportunities are currently not fully explored due to workload limitations?

When you buy or license content, what you pay for are the various ways to exploit that content. Thus, rights management is also fundamentally intertwined with financial management. It involves recording, tracking, and processing:

- contract payments to the seller or invoices to the seller

- when revenue recognition on the company's books can occur

- write-off/amortization of the content's cost over a period of time

- financial obligations to pay for specific content formats when delivering the content as part of a purchase or sale

- payments or "royalties" due to the seller when content is sold in a particular way

- profit sharing or "participations" due to the buyer that occur when content is sold in a particular way

The financial management of a content's contract and related rights is a complex feature of many rights management systems, and some offer off-the-shelf integrations to the most popular accounting systems to help companies manage that complexity in an automated, digitized way.

CURRENT AND FUTURE RIGHTS WORKFLOWS

Having identified the critical rights transactions, one must identify the stakeholders involved and the processes in which they work with rights. A mapping and analysis of the workflows involving rights will surface this information. These workflows could, for example, include the initial acquisition of content and rights and all the downstream process points at which a stakeholder uses the content or references the rights to that content. Mapping these workflows will be highly revealing. A company may discover all manner of inefficiencies and gaps that could be alleviated through more robust dissemination of rights information and process controls.

Most companies recognize they need digital workflows to be competitive. While striving for digital optimization, an organization should evaluate the current state of workflow digitization. Is the current digital workflow optimal? Or have manual workflows simply been recreated using automation and integration? Utilization and integration of rights, content, and asset management systems will together present opportunities for tremendous process transformation. Simply migrating manual steps into a digital interface is not likely to fully leverage the value of digitized capture, communication, and dissemination of rights and content.

As an organization designs a digital workflow, it must continue to predictively analyze the future workflows that may be needed in later phases or in the near future and their impact on staff and other resources. For instance, a fully realized digital workflow may reduce the workload of a legal team but create the need for additional staff in another team requiring new process steps to define and enter metadata.

DIGITAL SYSTEMS/TOOLS SURVEY

What digital tools and systems are currently in place, and what additional systems or capabilities could be added to the mix? Each organization faces a unique combination of factors—for example, complexity, budget, infrastructure, and staffing—that impact the degree of digitization that can be achieved. When considering which tools may be added to an existing infrastructure, one must consider the logistics of implementation and integration of those tools. Companies must commonly create phased roadmaps, with prerequisites and priorities to achieve a desired future state for digitized rights management. The tools available or potentially available are another complex but important piece of the DNA of digital strategy.

CODIFICATION OF RIGHTS INFORMATION INTO METADATA

Metadata fuels digitization and automation. Rights information cannot function as metadata if it remains in the long-form, narrative language of contracts. An organization must determine a method for the translation of vital contract language into standard metadata in order to achieve any digitized state. Analyzing contract and rights scenarios from this perspective will reveal which scenarios can be summarized or broken into discrete metadata points.

Currently, and unfortunately, not all content types have universally adopted standards for rights metadata. Where such standards are not adopted, as in the video media industries, their use would be a powerful advantage in increasing the velocity of rights dissemination within a company and to licensees and other third parties. As content contracts multiply due to the increasing dissection of content rights across partners, and the content distributors themselves compete and race across multiple distribution platforms at the same time, all participants involved are slowed by the lack of a common standard rights language that can be codified and automated between them. The needs for digital inter-operability between partnering companies will one day outweigh the main hurdles to establishing that standard:

- the extreme complexity of rights and associated metadata, particularly in the video industry among production companies, owners, and distributors

- the competitive industry model and other logistical challenges of establishing such a standard

- the resistance by some who perceive such a standard as a removal of competitive advantage in contract interpretation and not as a tool for more fully leveraging business opportunities

RISK TOLERANCE

As organizations move further away from the historical model of manual approval for every use of content, they must decide which usage scenarios are truly sensitive, risky, or nuanced enough to require the interjection in the digital workflow of a human judgment by a legal subject matter expert. These will continue to exist. Yet automation and digitization does not necessarily mean less security around rights information; quite often, with careful planning of systems and workflows, it will mean more security. As an organization holistically considers its workflows, available and future tools, and usage and transaction landscape, it can begin to make strategic decisions about its comfort level with automation. This can be as simple as having trained rights subject matter experts embedded within teams that consume rights for their exchanges and transactions. Or it can mean systematic display of "approved to view" rights in systems for users that need to see them.

RIGHTS MATURITY MODEL

A useful tool to examine where a company's rights management maturity state is and where it needs to be can be found in the Rights Maturity Model in Appendix C. The Rights Maturity Model was designed to create a matrix of rights functionality vis-a-vis a desired state of capability. At the intersection is a description of what functionality is found at a particular state. This is helpful, much like a map is, to see where a company is currently and where it anticipates it needs to go in the future. It can reveal new possibilities for rights functionalities and help stakeholders learn what is possible. It is recommended that this model be used, together with the rights and content workflow analysis, as the focus of a workshop with active workflow participants, managers, and their executives. Such a workshop would bring all parties to the table and provide important explanation of why rights are needed and by whom. Those insights and "ah-ha" moments about how a contract and its defined rights impact multiple systems, processes, and people will inform a digital transformation roadmap.

WHAT DOES AN OPTIMIZED DIGITAL ENVIRONMENT LOOK LIKE?

So what might all of this look like when it's put into practice? To illustrate the possibilities for transforming operations with digital rights management, we will examine two case studies from different ends of the content complexity spectrum.

CASE STUDY #1: PUBLISHING

In this case study, a publishing company uses photos and videos for its editorial and marketing output. Those assets are purchased for use in stories in magazines, used on the company's websites, posted on social media, and used in marketing materials to promote the company. The assets may be acquired in various ways, each requiring different rights. Lacking a dedicated RMS, the company opts to codify rights into metadata, to then be associated with the assets in DAM and CMS systems. The company analyzed its contracting scenarios and found the following:

1. Images and videos are purchased from stock agencies.

    • The company has limited rights and can only use each image for a single specific use.

2. Staff is assigned to take pictures and videos themselves.

    • The company owns the images outright and can use them in any way for all time.

3. Photographers and videographers are contracted to shoot exclusively for the magazine.

    • The company has broad but not exclusive rights to the assets, with limitations which vary per contract.

The very straightforward rights scenarios associated with scenarios #1 and #2 make for simple translation into metadata—essentially a yes or no setting for reuse of the assets. The more complex situation in scenario #3 presents a variety of possible rights, with varying opportunities for reuse of the relevant assets. Rights metadata for those assets would be in the form of a note describing the allowable reuse.

What happens when the contracting and purchase of content and rights occurs in a digital workflow? The legal team assigns the rights metadata, as above, manually into a contract management system. Integration of rights management system with the company's DAM system enables automatic creation placeholders for the assets as soon as a contract is signed. After the assets are delivered, they are manually ingested and added to the placeholders within the DAM system, and metadata from the contract management system automatically flows to the relevant assets through integration.

Configurations within the DAM and CMS systems set access privileges based on the rights metadata:

- Downloads are blocked for assets with no rights for reuse (scenario #1).

- Full access is allowed to assets the company owns outright (scenario #2).

- Access is granted only to specific teams for assets with limited rights (scenario #3).

In this case study, the company experiences real gains in automated access control by utilizing rights metadata and integrating the contract management system with DAM and CMS systems. In the future, the company's digital strategy could evolve to include a range of capabilities like automated asset ingest and delivery to print or web.

CASE STUDY #2:
TELEVISION PRODUCTION

A production company creates television shows and documentaries. They have a series in mind that they want to develop and sell, and it is pitched to several broadcast, cable, and Internet distributors. The series is approved for an outright sale to a cable network, and a contract is negotiated between the production company and the network. The process thus far—vetting of the content, negotiation of which rights are included in the sale, and price negotiations—

begins to take shape as a draft contract within a rights management system.

When both parties agree, the contract is executed. Critical details of the contract will include:

- the seller and buyer

- the content being sold

- the rights defining allowable usage

  - rights defined for a combination of criteria, including rights, distribution channels, term (period of time), territories, languages, and exclusivity

- the critical payments and invoice schedules tied to usage

  - participation payments to be paid back to the production company or other "participants" if it is sold in a certain way and what each of those payment definitions are

  - invoice schedule for when deliverables and their corresponding payments must be made

In a fully digital workflow, in which systems are integrated, the execution of the contract triggers system events along the rights management process. The execution date informs a scheduling department when it may air the program, it tells the inventory system or DAM that content is due to be delivered and triggers automated creation of a record in that system to await the digital file of the content, it informs production management systems how to schedule the work they need to do and in what order based on negotiated delivery dates, it tells the accounting system that revenue recognition can occur, and it informs sales systems if/when the content can be sold elsewhere through other distribution channels besides cable. Additionally, contract execution initiates the creation of the contract payment schedule—either in the rights management system to issue invoices via the company's accounting system or in the system that manages payment and amortization schedules.

After all of these rights-dependent actions and workflows are triggered, the robust digital environment maintains clarity about what can be done with the content after it is acquired. The rights metadata for each documentary episode in the series will also include rights for any externally sourced, or third party, materials used to make the documentary. Each of these materials will have its own contract. Third-party contracts could define rights for any or all of the following:

- images licensed to illustrate the story

- music

- narration

- video licensed from archives

- location releases for historical monuments or buildings

- personal releases for interviews with historical experts

There can be hundreds of such third-party elements and associated contracts. They are all interpreted and entered as metadata into the rights management system and related to the parent content. Even in this digital environment, much of that metadata entry is accomplished manually, while some metadata points are captured at the contracting stage and flow though systems from there. Rights metadata then flows with its related content throughout the content life cycle, triggering access and distribution controls and other rights-dependent behaviors.

This case study, up to this point, illustrates what is called "rights in," the collective processes involved with the acquisition of rights to content by an organization.

After acquiring and tagging content like the documentary in this example, the company will aim to license it to other organizations, gaining revenue through sales and royalties. An international salesperson tasked with selling content to foreign broadcast networks will use availability reports detailing what is available to be sold in her territory, during a period of time, in a particular language, etc. Such reports are the jewel in the crown of all rights management systems. Once content is legally cleared for sale, the contracting process begins again, this time with the licensee acquiring the content. There are additional financial considerations that now come into play. These include royalties defined for particular uses and the tracking and payment of participations, which the original network, the licensor, may have to make back to the production company. The licensee will need its own systems to track what is now its own content and rights. The collective processes involved with the selling or licensing of rights, and subsequent transactions are referred to as "rights out," where company is selling rights to its owned content out to another party in order to monetize it.

CONCLUSION

Rights management can run the gamut of a simple to a deeply complex endeavor. While companies are all different, rights are pervasive across processes and functions within any company working with content. Their deep interplay with sales, financial transactions, and distribution activities adds to their complexity. With the exponential proliferation of content, creators, distribution channels, consumers, and consumption tools, the need to optimize a digital strategy for rights management, regardless of company size, is more urgent with each passing day. Fortunately the tools available for managing rights have been increasing in variety of scale and sophistication as well. By taking thorough stock of current practices and future requirements, an organization can determine just how they need to pursue their digital optimization strategy. Digital transformation is being accomplished in whole or in part everywhere we turn. Rights management is a critical part of that transformation for companies that manage content. Profound, catalytic opportunities exist to proactively strategize, thoroughly utilize, and monetize content while controlling risk in a digitally integrated content ecosystem. Take these opportunities to speed the velocity of rights information across your enterprise so that your company is on the edge of innovative developments and can take advantage of your content's rights to meet them.

VIDEO RIGHTS MATURITY MODEL

With an understanding of video rights attributes and the considerations that impact rights usage in a company, we can establish a Video Rights Maturity Model. This model describes the definitional areas, or facets, essential to video rights maturity and the intersection of five defined levels of maturity for each facet. Complete the Video Rights Maturity Model Matrix assessment (on the following pages) by assessing your organization's level for each facet. As an organization matures, its level for the facets impacting its business will migrate from left to right on the maturity scale.

	Facet	Ad Hoc (1)	Incipient (2)
1	A controlled rights vocabulary is used.	Standard rights terms are not used across the organization or systems. Subject matter experts know the organization's rights vocabulary.	Standard rights terms are recognized as needed across the organization. Other groups and systems across the company have the need to understand critical rights terms.
2	System(s) exist to track rights for the video title asset.	Physical or digital copies of video contracts are manually evaluated by subject matter experts to determine the rights for a video title asset on request.	The organization finds manual evaluation of contracts unwieldy and identifies the need for video title asset level rights to be systematically managed.
3	System(s) exist to track rights at the parent video title asset and its third-party assets' rights.	Third-party asset contracts for a video asset are manually calculated and summarized, along with the video asset's rights.	Third-party asset contracts for a video title asset can no longer be manually calculated and summarized with efficiency. The organization identifies the need for third-party asset contracts to be calculated systematically.
4	Timely availability reporting within a time window exists.	Availability reporting requires a large staff of people or systems effort to perform.	Availability reporting is understood to take too long to perform to meet company needs. Systematic availability reporting requirements are in definition or iteration.
5	Timely "Why Not" availability reporting within a time window exists.	A company manually researches why a video is not available for requested right attribute(s).t.	A company identifies that it cannot effectively manage manually researching why a video is not available. Systematic "Why Not" availability reporting requirements are in definition or iteration.
6	Rights attributes and information is understood and shared to allow the timely dissemination of rights information across the company.	Video rights information is diffused; interpreted and distributed by anyone in the organization who has access to the video contract.	Video rights information is beginning to organize and centralize. The need for an authenticated video rights systems of record is recognized.

Formative (3)	Operational (4)	Optimizing (5)
controlled rights vocabulary is eing evaluated for the people and stems that need them.	A controlled rights vocabulary is implemented across people and systems that need them.	A controlled rights vocabulary is integrated and operational across the organization. There is governance and iteration for the vocabulary and processes to re-evaluate Rights attributes as change occurs. The company drives support for an industry standard video vocabulary and schema.
he organization is implementing upgrading outdated systems to ack video title asset rights.	The organization has systems and interfaces to track video title asset rights across critical workflows. Video title asset rights are available to those who need them.	The organization has systems to track video title asset rights and is continually evaluating best practices (processes or systems) to send video title asset rights to those who need them.
he organization is implementing upgrading outdated systems track third-party asset rights ong with the video title asset vel rights.	Third-party asset rights are calculated with the video title asset rights to deliver the full rights availability for a video asset.	The organization has systems to track third-party asset rights along with the video title asset's rights. It is continually evaluating best practices (processes or systems) to ingest or communicate expiring third party rights to those who need this information.
vailability reporting is being implemented for systems, improving rocesses and workflows.	Availability reporting runs efficiently and rights information flows to people and systems to meet company-wide needs.	Availability reporting is proactively improved and automated to accommodate system changes, new lines of business, and market change. Processes exist to leverage availability reporting for predictive creative, sales, and distribution growth.
Why Not" availability reporting being implemented for systems, nproving processes and workows.	"Why Not" availability reporting runs efficiently, and rights information flows to people and systems to meet company-wide needs for renegotiation or renewal of expired content.	"Why Not" availability reporting is proactively improved and automated to accommodate system changes, new lines of business, and market change. Processes exist to leverage "Why Not" availability reporting for predictive creative, sales, and distribution growth.
ideo rights management is organized and centralized in system\s record by rights management bject matter experts who are sponsible for answering video ghts questions for the entire mpany.	Video rights are based on a company's standard rights vocabulary, are organized into systems of record by rights management subject matter experts and are disseminated across the company to internal consumers trained in understanding their critical video rights data.	Rights management is based on an industry standard video rights vocabulary that is widely understood, visible within the company, and is evangelized with its partners.

	Facet	Ad Hoc (1)	Incipient (2)
7	Rights information flows systematically from acquisition to delivery.	Video rights information is managed manually within business siloes, its entry is duplicated in various systems that are not integrated across the workflows that depend on rights.	Video rights is understood to require a rights management system and initial reporting is used to pass video rights information to others that need it. Duplicative rights data entry across systems still exists.
8	Digital rights management is implemented.	Tracking of distributed digital video content is done manually or via distribution systems' reporting. When litigation causes the retrieval of content, the retrieval process is manual via email, etc. The ability to monitor and retrieve video used outside of the rights attributes granted does not exist.	Tracking of distributed digital video content is done manually or via distribution systems' reporting and is unwieldy and unreliable due to volume of content and\or number of distributors. The company identifies its ability to control its distributed content is a risk.
9	Rights systems are integrated with internal financial systems.	Video rights contractual milestone payment schedules, participations, or royalties definitions are manually re-entered into other systems to calculate these obligations.	Video rights contractual milestone payments schedules, participations, or royalties definitions are manually re-entered into other systems to calculate these obligations. It is understood that this is duplicative t video rights entry being performed in rights management systems.
10	Rights systems support external partners in self-service reporting.	External partner questions or reporting for contractual payments including gross or net sales, participations, or royalties is performed manually on some frequency.	External partner questions or reporting for contractual payments including gross or net sales, participations, or royalties is partially systematized and can be communicated to the partne

Formative (3)	Operational (4)	Optimizing (5)
ideo rights are stored in a rights management system and some ritical interfaces supporting core orkflows exist. The potential for urther automation exists.	Core video rights information is integrated across key business systems that require them, enabling video rights self-service, some search and discovery of available content.	Highly automated internal video rights processes exist to speed the search, discovery, distribution, and digital rights management of a company's videos.
digital rights management system is identified as necessary and reliminary implementation exists or core metadata and video term nd dates. It is possible to more usily report and find content out f license, although this is still a artially manual exercise.	A digital rights management system is implemented and core rights attributes are embedded in the digital video file. Timed watermarking, self-destruction, or other methods are available to disable the content past contractual term end date.	Digital rights management is seen to require industry and technology efforts to enforce the use of video content based on term end dates but also on other granted rights attributes. The ability to withdraw or disable the content outside those granted attributes become possible.
ideo rights management systems r their integrated financial ystems partially inform or are informed by systems or interfaces to neet contractual payments, royalies, or participations processes.	Video rights contractual milestone payment schedules, participations, or royalties definitions are calculated within rights management systems or fed to financial systems to calculate these obligations.	Video rights management systems, in addition to fully automated contractual financial processing, inform or are informed by automated partner royalties or participations feeds or interfaces
xternal partner questions or reorting for contractual payments ncluding gross or net sales, parcipations, or royalties is mostly ystematized. Some reporting may e self-service, online.	External partner questions or reporting for contractual payments including gross or net sales, participations, or royalties is fully systematized. Reporting is self-service, online.	External partner questions or reporting for contractual payments including gross or nets, participations, or royalties is fully systematized and relies entirely on a standard rights vocabulary and common reporting templates. Core reporting is self-service, online.

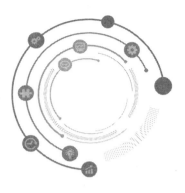

CHAPTER 8

CONSIDERATIONS FOR DIGITAL CONTENT WORKFLOW DESIGN

by Holly Boerner

Implicit to working with digital content is the work itself—the processes involved in how digital content is made, revised, approved, distributed, stored, accessed, reinvented, and so on, as digital information and assets wind their way through enterprise environments, out to the world, and back. This introduces the challenge of understanding what needs to be done by whom, using what, to manage content throughout its life cycle, and in a way that drives monetary return while mitigating risk and managing resource waste. In short, it introduces the need for smart, optimized *workflows* for managing digital content.

When thinking workflow, it's easy to zero in on the resources and processes that guide content's work-in-progress (WIP) trajectory—who are the teams and departments, and what are the technology applications, systems, and tools they use to ensure something digital is created, approved, and optimally poised for use? In reality, though, workflows intersect with content no matter what its life-cycle stage. Regardless of whether digital content is at a WIP, final state/live, or inactive life-cycle point, understanding the intersections of people and technology unique to each phase is key to ensuring that workflow processes will support, and not hinder, content's smart, efficient utilization. Meeting this goal will confirm that streamlined, user-friendly workflows are enacted and that they allow necessary process actions to be taken while meeting deadline requirements.

WORKFLOW AND DIGITAL CONTENT LIFE-CYCLE PHASES

ELEMENTS OF WORKFLOW SPECIFIC TO LIFE-CYCLE PHASES

The life cycle of digital content is rarely linear, but as content is invented, used, repurposed, and reused, it is possible to identify three broad life-cycle stages that content passes through: *work in progress (WIP), final state/live,* and *inactive.* Each life-cycle phase should be understood according to its defining characteristics, and when designing a phase's workflows, priority should be given to addressing the unique requirements and activities specific to that phase. Failure to understand and address process needs according to unique life-cycle requirements will likely introduce a "square-peg/round-hole" scenario that in turn can introduce inefficiencies, compliance risk, and resource waste.

1. **Work in Progress (WIP):** As previously identified, WIP content often jumps to the forefront when considering digital content workflows and for good reason. The broadest, arguably most intricate parts of digital content's life cycle are often those encompassing its creation, production, and approval processes. These activities may require attention from a variety of teams and departments within an enterprise and require a wide array of technology applications, systems, and tools to execute workflow actions in relation to digital content. The main activities defining WIP workflow processes include:

    - *Creation and Revision*—the creation and revision of digital content elements (creative file, document, or even piece of information), either simple (a single element) or complex (a compound document containing information and assets).

    - *Storage and Routing*—methods of storing and sharing digital elements within and across an environment, potentially extending to external parties

    - *Review and Approval*—methods of viewing and/or interacting with a digital element to annotate, reject, and/or approve it.

    - *Iteration Tracking*—the tracking of digital elements' iterations as they proceed through development.

Iteration tracking assumes multiple and alternative versions of content are under consideration, typically simultaneously.

2.   **Final State/Live:** Once digital content has passed through its creation/production phase, it can typically be considered "final" and ready for live use. At this stage, activities surrounding the shepherding of digital content encompass:

- *Search and Retrieval*—Finding and accessing digital content is a fundamental step toward its utilization. The workflows around this, though, may vary depending on whether content is brand new, having just emerged from the WIP process, or is long-existing and requires resurfacing for reference, reuse, or repurposing. Also influential in determining search and retrieval workflow paths is the source housing the digital content. Whether something is internally held by the organization or externally held by a third party will influence the speed, methodologies, and tools necessary for obtaining said content.

- *Distribution and Utilization*—On accessing, digital content will need to be distributed across the channels in which it will serve its functional purpose. Depending on digital content's nature, the channels and forms in which it is used may feel just short of infinite—so a wide variety of distribution processes and requirements should be anticipated.

3. **Inactive:** Finally, digital content will likely be seen as having a formal or informal expiration date, after which its importance to an organization diminishes. Triggers for this may range from soft reasons like changing styles or cultural mood, to needing to proactively retire or purge digital content to maintain compliance or mitigate liabilities. Inactive content should not be seen to be in an irrevocable "end-of-life" state, though, as business rhythms may require once-inactive content to be reactivated for reuse or repurposing in a new way. Thus, workflows facilitating inactive content typically involve:

    - *Search and Retrieval*—Locating and acquiring content will be a fundamental action in the lifespan of inactive content, similar to final state/live content.

    - *Routing and Retrieval*—Once found, content will intrinsically go through a specific routing and approval process as a means of being deactivated or activated.

    - *Archiving and Deleting*—Digital content will be finally archived or purged.

ELEMENTS OF WORKFLOW RELEVANT TO ALL LIFE-CYCLE PHASES

In addition to the activities characteristically in play per life-cycle stage, some elements and actions will influence content workflow at all life-cycle stages:

- *Access Permissions*—A critical determinant in digital content workflows will be facilitating who needs to do what, with what, through what mechanism, when. During WIP phases, this will likely be dictated by the need to create, access, view, revise, approve, and/ or share digital content to keep it moving through its production cycle. For final state and inactive phases, basic access to, or restrictions from, content will be major determinations influencing who can and will need to obtain, share, or hide content in relation to business policies and requirements.

- *Workflow Ownership and User Roles*—It is important that all workflows are assigned an owner that becomes responsible for collaborating in workflow design, maintaining the workflow by continually assessing efficacy, soliciting user feedback, and assigning user roles for specific steps. Assigning specific roles and responsibilities to each step of the workflow places clear ownership for completion of each task of any digital content workflow from WIP to inactive life-cycle stages.

- *Version Tracking and Identification*—This should be considered to sit at a level above the *iteration tracking* specific to WIP workflows, to consider alternate content versions that may be produced and/or used pending variance of date, region, language, or content quality (i.e., size, format, etc.).

- *Content Categorization*—Categorizing content is a fundamental workflow action that occurs across life-cycle stages, as the resulting classifications will serve to define both what content is and what is done with it. Classifiers bridging descriptive, technical, and administrative themes will arguably play the fundamental role in determining the how, when, and where of workflow activity in relation to digital content.

CONSIDERATIONS FOR BUILDING DIGITAL CONTENT WORKFLOWS

Understanding that workflows will need to facilitate unique activities and requirements per life-cycle stage is an important initial layer to unpack in designing workflows for digital content. But actually building workflows requires taking this understanding one step further to consider how business policies and requirements, human touch points, and technology tools all intersect to facilitate efficient, easy-to-perform digital content workflows.

BUSINESS RULES, REQUIREMENTS, AND POLICIES

Business requirements and policies can be considered the core framework defining the scope of all workflow design. This encompasses a wide landscape anticipating how general influencers like budget, head count, and deadlines will dictate parameters within which workflows must operate. And while these elements are broadly defined, their specific impact can sometimes present as granular or idiosyncratic constraints—for example, the impact of requiring use of particular data transfer systems to meet compliance rules or record management policies dictating storage locations and retention schedules for content.

TECHNOLOGY

Technology systems, applications, and tools play a critical role in facilitating workflows, to the point that their deployment can make or break workflow logic and efficiency. It can be easy to look to technology as a magic button solution to "just do workflow," but in reality, the strategic deployment of technology can be one of the most complicated workflow nuts to crack. Keeping key considerations in mind when determining how to leverage technology will go far in ensuring it's deployed to enable, and not hinder, efficient content flows.

- *Automation vs. Manual Actions*—Technology systems, applications, and/or tools are often utilized for the advantage they offer in automating workflow activities. However, this potential should be approached with a commitment toward understanding and balancing when automations can help streamline and speed up workflow steps and when they run the risk of over-engineering a task. Automations are typically most helpful when scaled to what needs to be accomplished. For example, this may be seen in back-end processes that bridge systems, enable end-to-end actions, and establish a technological ecosystem of facilitation. Alternatively, automations may be small batch processes that are manually triggered by human touch points capable of knowing when an automation provides efficiency and when it would be a too-heavy hand.

- *Flexible Process Paths*—When technology systems are deployed as full-fledged process management systems, it is critical to approach their configuration as a balancing act. Technology is commonly assumed to provide value in aligning workflow paths, standardizing a potentially fragmented range of processes into a defined, predictable flow. These scenarios rightly and intentionally introduce efficiency through standardization but in doing so remove the potential for human touch points and intervention that may be necessary to manage exceptions. Technology should support people's inherent creativity and abilities to discern the optimal ways of completing a task for a particular context. Technology-facilitated workflows should anticipate this transaction when being designed to ensure the right level of system management is set.

- *The Right-Fit Tool for the Job*—Ultimately, technology is a tool capable of assisting human actions for the sake of accomplishing a desired outcome. Like any tool deployed to accomplish a task, logic dictates one match the tool to the task—why use a hammer when a screwdriver is needed? But in enterprise environments where multitiered workflows connect cyclical, interwoven flows of content, identifying the right tool for the job can become tricky. This is especially so when vendor marketing presents technology solutions as Swiss Army Knife applications, capable of doing anything and everything an enterprise may need. When considering the right-fit technology tool for a workflow, organizations should be shrewd in considering what technology is appropriate to use how—when it's appropriate to stretch an application beyond its primary purpose and when such extensions may inhibit process efficiencies. Realistically, few organizations will have the resources to invest in a full suite of tools all individually and ideally tuned to meet each discrete workflow action. Still, it is dangerous to be cavalier in deploying technology to perform functions it is not well engineered to do.

PEOPLE

Finally, the other critical factor to consider in workflow design is the people performing the tasks:

- *Identifying Genuine Requirements vs. Naturalized Habits*—Apart from the unique occasions when a business or process is truly new to an organization, workflows are rarely conceived from scratch but are instead often evolved from existing methods of completing an activity. Evolving workflows can be a major or minor undertaking impacting teams' practices, but its first step involves determining what action must be executed. This is typically diagnosed by identifying the *what* of *how* something is currently completed, and this can be challenging. Parsing the core of *what* a task accomplishes from the *methods* in which it is accomplished can be difficult. But this difference is critical, as a task's purpose will define the business requirement, while the methodology will present opportunities for reinvention and thus improvement. When building workflows, it is important to be discerning of this difference to prevent carrying inefficiencies forward and to ensure optimization opportunities are developed out of methodological opportunities that don't mistakenly discard actual process requirements.

- *Influence of the Consumer Digital Experience*—In considering digital content workflows, it would be irresponsible not to draw connections to the constant, everyday experiences people have using consumer-level digital technology. These experiences set expectations for how easy, fast, and intuitive "something" should be to accomplish via a digital tool. Many digital content workflow activities—search, retrieval, acquisition, distribution—are everyday actions in the consumer sphere, and therefore ease-of-execution standards for their enterprise counterparts will be approached with the same level of expectation. This presents an opportunity for organizations to learn from consumer practices and even leverage digital fluencies taught by the consumer sphere. But it also sets a high bar that people will expect to see answered when tasked with performing actions whose methodologies are defined in the easy-to-use, intuitive consumer space.

- *Need for Workaround-Proof Workflows*—People are different from technology in that if a workflow doesn't "work," people won't stop what they're doing and spit out an error message (at least not most of the time). People are smart, creative, and typically committed to getting the job done—so if a workflow doesn't work, people will find a way to work around it. Causes for failed workflows can be myriad—inefficient steps or technology requirements may inhibit the ability to meet a deadline. Or, as just described, a lack of intuitive, user-friendly tools may drive people to leverage other available tools in ways they shouldn't be used. People will use what they can to get the job done in a timely manner—whether driven by speed-of-business requirements or simply to accomplish something in the easiest way possible. For better or worse, workflows must be designed with this common denominator in mind or risk a failure of adoption and in turn a failure to comply with policies, standards, and regulations that workflows were intended to ensure.

CONCLUSION

The process of how digital content is produced, flows through an environment, and gets utilized in the world is an intricate, multilayered scenario that requires many tiers of consideration to be enacted well. The intersection of content's life-cycle phases, technology tools for facilitation, and people performing tasks must be holistically understood. By doing so, efficient, logical, easy-to-execute workflow paths can be enacted and pave the way for optimized digital content use and monetization, all while mitigating risk.

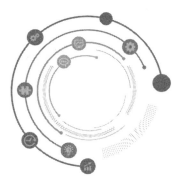

CHAPTER 9

INFORMATION GOVERNANCE

by John Horodyski

The word *governance* is often misunderstood as a set of rules, when in fact it actually refers to practices of organization as well as processes for interaction and decision making. *Governance is good; in fact, it is great.* Governance, and specifically IT governance, is defined as "putting structure around how organizations align IT strategy with business strategy, ensuring that companies stay on track to achieve their strategies and goals, and implementing good ways to measure IT's performance. It makes sure that all stakeholders' interests are taken into account and that processes provide measurable results."[7] In corporations, IT departments have long used governance as a monitoring mechanism to drive results, manage risk,

---

7 "IT Governance Definition and Solutions," Karen D. Schwartz, CIO, May 22, 2007, http://www.cio.com/article/111700/IT_Governance_Definition_and_Solutions.

and meet user expectations for the complex interrelationships of diverse systems. Today, as the information landscape extends afield to include content management, records management, digital asset management, and knowledge management, the need for information governance has become a strategic imperative. In this scenario, information governance, while often practiced in collaboration *with* information technology, should be understood as not driven explicitly *by* IT but rather pursued as a holistic, corporate objective. Developing a governance model—as a document, set of rules, or standard operating procedure—requires practices and processes that can be sustained to deliver ROI, innovation, and collaboration.

Participation from all levels of the organization is key. In particular, engaging the leadership by involving them in the big decisions, holding regular reviews, and keeping them talking about DAM will yield the greatest benefits from DAM. IT governance is the best way to manage change, from implementation to maintenance of the technology itself. However, we have reached a time in our history when we must implement information governance in order to move our information into the future. This is something that is both more holistic and more specific than IT governance, and it needs to address the data and information throughout your organization. Information governance is the structure around how organizations align information management, beginning with metadata, taxonomy, policy development, stewardship, and technology, to serve the creation, use, and distribution of information.

The governance structure establishes:

- strategic leadership

- organizational practices

- management processes

Good information governance starts with a project charter, working committee, and predetermined timeline *at the inception* of any new system implementation or corporate initiative. While the governance policy may establish rules and measurement tools, the ultimate goal is to create unbreakable, collaborative connections between people, process, technology, and content. Achieving collective solutions requires the participation of people from all levels of the organization. Everyone engaged with the content will have a different perspective, so giving voice to diverse views through recurring review and feedback sessions increases engagement and empowers content to work for the entire organization.

Content management, records management, digital asset management, and knowledge management—all elements of a larger information management practice—evolve over time. A governance strategy can manage change while mitigating risk by gaining operational and intellectual control of digital assets and information. Adopting a digital strategy in conjunction with leveraging technology solutions will enable the organization to react to change without being thrown off course. Creating a solution for governing information and connecting it throughout the business means that assets can generate revenue, increase efficiencies, and meet new and emerging market opportunities.

PEOPLE, PROCESS, AND TECHNOLOGY ... AND CONTENT

Ultimately, information governance is the structure enabling content stewardship, beginning with metadata and taxonomy strategy, policy development, and technology solutions to serve the creation, use, and distribution of information. Information and content do not emerge fully formed into the world. They are products of *people* working with *technology* in the execution of a *process*. Proper governance of information and content must include a detailed review and analysis of all factors involved in their manifestation and life cycles, including organization, workflow, rights, and preservation. Optimity recommends considering the following practices and processes as a roadmap for sustainable information governance.

ORGANIZATIONAL PRACTICES

Every organization has a different culture and will likely adopt different strategies for applying information governance practices. However, all users appreciate using systems that reflect their needs and workflow practices. Content that is governed and maintained by the following practices will produce measurable ROI by increasing intrinsic content value, lowering risk, and sustaining efficiency:

1. **Apply Metadata**—Develop a schema that includes the descriptive, administrative, and structural information about assets and information.

    - **Descriptive metadata** describes a resource for purposes of discovery and identification (i.e., information you would use in a search). It can include elements such as title, creator, author, and content-related keywords.

    - **Structural metadata** indicates how compound elements are configured, for example how a digital image is composed as provided in EXIF data or how pages are ordered to form chapters. It can include elements such as file format, file dimension, and file size.

- **Administrative metadata** provides information that helps manage an asset. Two common subsets of administrative data are rights management metadata (which deals with intellectual property rights) and preservation metadata (which contains information needed to archive and preserve a resource).

2. **Define Controlled Vocabularies**—Controlled vocabularies can be used for drop-downs and pick lists. Employing a predefined list of terms for the most important aspects of content is a good way to provide authority and consistency when applying metadata to assets. For example, if the location of an asset is an important informational element, then a controlled vocabulary defining country names would make sense.

3. **Establish a Retention Policy**—Content owners should create a **retention policy** and **retention schedule** that quantifies information or asset life cycle and defines the relevance of a given asset type over time. Identifying what is ephemeral, duplicative, or low value decreases system burden while allowing the focus to be on preservation of archival, unique, and reusable material. Periodically updating the retention policy and schedule is also an important practice.

4. **Create a Taxonomy**—By creating classification hierarchies, content can be organized by its interrelationships. The best reason for creating and implementing a single, standard, scalable taxonomy across the enterprise is that it provides good business value, enhancing and improving enterprise search and serendipitous discovery.

MANAGEMENT PROCESSES

Management is about execution, coordination, and implementation of results and requires attention to detail as well as follow-up. Applying these management processes to the master information governance strategy provides a structure for stakeholders to both interact with and influence content stored in the system for maximum performance results.

1. **Appoint a Governance Council**—The council will align processes, requirements, and controls comprised of core stakeholders across different departments and varying entitlement levels within an organization. As systems and initiatives evolve, the council can communicate changes and developments across the user base and provide support for new ideas and initiatives.

2. **Assign Decision Rights and Accountability**—While a collective decision-making process is critical in governance, there must also be an approval process that mitigates the risk of allowing ad hoc or quick fixes to systems or organizational structures. Uncoordinated management over time can destroy structure and lead to costly remediation of problems.

3. **Assemble a Stewardship Network**—The responsibility to elevate a change to the governance council or implement a change in metadata, for example, can be delegated to a network of stewards who serve as representatives for individual departments. Stewards can facilitate change management for updates, be the

conduit for communications, and collect system and user performance metrics.

4. **Anticipate the Need for Issue Resolution**—Engagement from all stakeholders requires confidence that individual ideas will be heard. Formalize change requests for any adjustments to system functionality or initiative strategy. Requests should be formally submitted via *change request forms* made available to users and, if necessary, subject to review.

5. **Collaborate with IT**—Content management systems within an organization rarely exist in a vacuum. Other systems may interact with CMS, DAM, RM, or KM solutions and offer similar functionality. Involving IT in governance will ensure that content management systems are aligned within the larger technology ecosystem and will provide support for tasks like vendor management as well. Involving IT also provides the opportunity to educate people accustomed to running the machines on the priorities for *managing what's inside* the machine.

6. **Establish Communication Channels**—The value of maintaining recurring communications with stakeholders cannot be overstated. Schedule regular meetings to hear direct, unfiltered insights and gather feedback from user groups. These often result in innovation and the development of new business opportunities for the system.

7. **Review Metadata and Taxonomy**—The only constant in business is change, and mechanisms for leveraging metadata terms and taxonomy structures must have the ability to reflect evolving business realities. Beyond checking accuracy and authenticity, consider the effect of database and workflow changes on schemas and taxonomy. Political sensitivities within an organization or changes to the competitive landscape can influence descriptive metadata's relevance. Monitor the effectiveness of search terms in the user interface, and make sure that they contribute to, rather than hinder, navigation. It is also important to document changes to all master metadata governance documentation to make sure specifications are up to date and relevant.

CONCLUSION

Managing information is not a project; it is a program. To achieve true governance, all of the interconnected elements must be considered. The application of these suggested organizational practices and management processes require considerable attention at all stages and by all stakeholders. However, the health of the governance practice is one of the most telling indicators and accurate predictors of enterprise information management success. Every organization needs a way to ensure that the creation, use, and distribution of information sustain the organization's strategies and objectives. Governance is the best way to increase and expand the benefits and returns of all information assets.

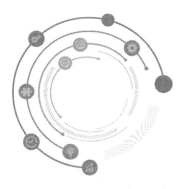

CHAPTER 10

RETURN ON INVESTMENT

by Rory Tierney, Chad Beer, and Gareth Harper

ROI, or return on investment, is a term often thrown around in the context of any costly overhaul of procedures. This is true in information management as much as any business area, where those holding the purse strings are often reluctant to invest in new personnel, software, or systems unless they can see the value of their expenditure. Frequently, however, the meaning of the term ROI is left implicit, and the support for an investment in new systems consists of a rough business case based largely on anecdotal evidence. In this chapter, we dig deeper into the meaning of ROI and how ROI analysis can help inform investment decisions as well as provide greater insight into how well current systems are functioning.

We begin by defining return on investment itself, from both an economic and a financial perspective, and then look at how ROI applies to the information management world. We then present a logical structure for breaking down costs and benefits into their component parts and performing an ROI analysis.

What does *return on investment* mean?

Many are familiar with the phrase *return on investment* in a financial setting. An investor buys a financial product, such as shares in a company, with the expectation (or hope!) that the value of those shares will rise. When they choose to sell, any profit made on top of the initial investment (through increases in the price of the asset plus any capital gain) constitutes the return.

In a non-financial business context, the logic is the same, although the mechanism may be different. Investment is required to start a company, with the aim of producing goods or services to be sold. The profit created constitutes the return on investment. Existing companies, too, will make investments to become more efficient, diversify into new areas of business, or attract talented employees. All of these investments are made to generate returns, either directly or indirectly.

We can in fact expand the notion of return beyond purely monetary returns. If a company invests in employee wellness, for example, this may be with the aim of improving productivity and thus increasing revenue. However, there is also some intrinsic value in improved health for employees that may be completely separate from any productivity gains—improved health for existing employees, reputational benefits, and attractiveness of the company to potential new employees. Depending on the perspective of the employer, these factors could also be considered part of the return on an investment.

In colloquial terms, therefore, whenever we speak about *value for money* we are speaking about return on investment. But it is useful to define two complementary measures: *financial return on investment* and *economic return on investment.*

Financial ROI is the narrower of the two measures and focuses on the bottom line. Only "cashable" returns—money saved and money gained—are counted. Economic ROI is a broader term that includes value that isn't necessarily cashable: these can be intangible gains that are hard to quantify, like morale or benefits that might not necessarily lead to a direct cash saving but have a value, like saving employee time (assuming that time is reallocated to other work).

Finally, one of the reasons it is important to think about ROI is because of the notion of *opportunity cost.* This concept reflects the fact that whenever a decision is made, it excludes any alternative that could have been chosen. The opportunity cost is the cost of the next best alternative that is given up. For instance, allocating an existing employee to carry out a new task represents an investment: the cost is equivalent to what they could be doing otherwise. Similarly, while an investor is looking to avoid losing money and to make money, they are also looking to optimize their investment—to get the most value possible from any expenditure. Opportunity cost comes in here—as well as asking whether an investment is worth the money, it is important to consider on what else the money could be spent.

ROI IN THE WORLD OF INFORMATION MANAGEMENT

The rest of this book illustrates some of the many reasons why good information management is important, as well as highlighting why incoherent or overly complex systems can be problematic. At a high level, investing in information management—whether by buying and implementing a new system or devoting time and effort to optimize processes—seems something of a no-brainer. But at a more detailed level it can be difficult to determine just how much to spend and what it will achieve. Why is this? Information management is a multifaceted practice, involving technology, people, and processes. Within an organization, IM will touch many different teams and workflows. Investments are often shared by several parties. Returns can occur at various points in an asset's life cycle and can be difficult to capture. Identifying all of the points of investment and return is challenging in itself. Assigning value to them, and potentially putting a dollar value on them, only adds to that challenge.

Let's look more closely at investments, through the lens of a fictional case study. In this scenario we have a company that uses photos for packaging materials and is exploring purchasing a system for managing them. There are various investments that must be accounted for, such as in the assets themselves, in the system, and in the time required of the people involved. (While discussing assets in this example, these examples can be extrapolated and applied to all manner of information, records, and artifacts.) Similarly, there are a range of potential benefits of the new system, including:

- direct cost savings (in images, equipment, etc.)

- time savings through greater efficiency

- greater asset utilization

- risk reduction

- boosted morale

While these can be identified pretty quickly at a high level, making an informed decision as to whether this represents a "good" investment (Taking opportunity cost into account, is it better than the next best alternative use of that money?) requires mapping out both the explicit costs (like investing in new hardware) and the implicit costs (like people's time) as well as identifying, mapping out, and ideally quantifying the benefits. The next section describes a logical structure for doing so.

THE LOGIC MODEL

The logic model presented here is a framework for analyzing the impact and return on investment of a program, through separating out the costs and benefits of a given activity or set of activities. The model, and its use in evaluating ROI, was developed by the UK's National Audit Office for the evaluation of government spending plans.[8]

As an example, imagine a car factory. The function of the car factory is building cars—at the highest level, that is the activity performed in the factory. With this in mind, we can begin sketching out the remainder of the logic model structure. It takes activities as the central focus and asks: What is needed to carry out the activity, what is used to carry out the activity, what is produced by the activity, and what does that achieve? It is expressed as follows:

RESOURCES — INPUTS — ACTIVITIES — OUTPUTS — OUTCOMES

---

8 National Audit Office, "Assessing value for money," accessed Jan. 22, 2016, https://www.nao.org.uk/successful-commissioning/general-principles/value-for-money/assessing-value-for-money/

Resources represent the assets and equipment required to carry out the building of the car. These are likely to be the factory itself, equipment within the factory, and the factory's employees.

Inputs represent what those resources use to carry out the activity. These are the raw materials used to build the car, such as steel, rubber, glass, and paint.

Activities, as mentioned, are what's actually done—the building of the car.

Outputs represent what is produced: in this case, a car.

Outcomes relate this back to the purpose of the activities— what is gained from building a car? This is predominantly likely to be profit maximization through revenue gains but may also include such things as meeting consumer demand, improved market share, and shareholder returns.

The advantage of separating out these individual "components" of the act of building a car is the ease of identifying costs and benefits. Resources carry a cost (the cost of the factory, the cost of employing people to build cars, the cost of maintaining equipment), and inputs may carry a cost (in this case, the cost of raw materials). Activities, as mentioned, are the central focus, through which resources, input, output, and outcomes are measured. Output and outcomes represent benefits, i.e., the value created.

We can repeat the same exercise for our fictional company's use of photos. The activity in this case could be producing images for packaging materials (with all that entails—sourcing and editing images, integrating them into packaging design, creating mock-ups, etc.). Working from the center out, the inputs are the raw images—

purchased, commissioned, or created in-house. The outputs are the use of the selected and edited images on packaging materials. The resources, therefore, are whatever is needed to turn those inputs into outputs: the people responsible, the hardware and software they use, and their office space. The outcome relates back to the purpose of using those images: to improve the packaging materials and potentially to sell more products.

With this in mind, we can begin to understand the cost of the process and its benefits by mapping out and quantifying what currently happens (the "current state" or baseline). What does creating images cost? How much time is spent on editing photos? What is the value of having quality images on a company's packaging? But this is not yet an ROI analysis until we compare this current scenario with an alternative.

By repeating the logic model exercise for an alternative state and comparing this to the baseline, we can map out what is likely to change under the new system the company is considering. Importantly, while the types of resources, inputs, and outputs are unlikely to change, the amounts may differ. Introducing a new activity— checking a new centralized library of images before commissioning or creating new ones—may carry an increased resource cost (the digital library itself and the people maintaining it) but could save people's time in creating or searching for images (a resource saving), as well as save on the cost of purchasing new images (an input saving), and could result in better quality images being used (an improvement in outputs and potentially outcomes). Of course, by changing or introducing a new activity, other activities in the company's process or workflow may also be changed, and new or different resources and inputs may be required.

The logic model for the alternative state should also include the resources, inputs, and activities required to achieve the new state from the current baseline (i.e., the investments required to get there).

When comparing two scenarios, the logic model allows assessment of four key concepts:

1. **Economy:** The relative cost of two options can be assessed by looking at the resources and inputs required.

2. **Efficiency:** This represents the relationship between outputs and the resources and inputs required. If you can achieve more outputs with the same resources and inputs, or the same outputs with fewer resources and inputs, you are more efficient.

3. **Effectiveness:** This represents the relationship between outcomes and the resources and inputs required. You could be very efficient at producing outputs, but if these do not achieve the goals or purposes of the whole enterprise, it is not effective. The outcomes achieved by the resources and inputs represent effectiveness.

4. **Cost effectiveness**, or ROI, represents the three previous concepts taken as a whole, relating outcomes back to the original investment.

ROI ANALYSIS

For an individual or organization, setting out—or even just thinking through—the logic model is a good place to start. It provides a framework through which the differences in costs and benefits between two scenarios can be identified. In order to complete an analysis, though, these differences need to be measured and valued.

Let's take the inputs from our fictional company as an example. Suppose the implementation of a new content or digital asset management system cuts down the number of new images that need to be used to create the same or superior outputs as the previous system. This can be identified from the logic model.

But we also need to measure how many fewer images need to be purchased or created, which can be tricky to do if the new system is not yet in place. A proxy could be derived from other companies' experience, a pilot program could be put in place, or best estimates could be derived from speaking to users of the current system. Depending on how images are sourced, it could also be easier to measure this in terms of fewer photo shoots, fewer stock image purchases, or less time spent creating images in-house, rather than arriving at a number of images estimate. While these approaches necessarily result in an estimate, figures can be verified against reality once implementation of the new system begins. (For a retrospective ROI analysis, or one taking place during implementation, this figure can be assessed more accurately, and a post-implementation review is an important step in the ROI process.)

Next, the value of this reduction must be assessed. For those assets that are created in commissioned photo or video shoots, the cost is pretty simple to capture. A shoot costs a given amount and results in a specific number of images. One can easily determine the price per asset. Similarly, some assets may come from stock agencies, representing another direct cost. However, some assets may be created in-house by staff. Reduction of the need for these does not represent a direct financial saving (assuming those employees are retained) and thus wouldn't be captured in a financial ROI analysis.

But if employees are reallocated to other work, it does represent an economic saving and would be captured in an economic ROI analysis.[9]

This is, simply, because the time spent creating images carries an opportunity cost—the next best use of that time. By freeing up this time, employees are able to carry out tasks they would otherwise not have done, including tackling new or additional business opportunities—potentially leading to a "domino effect" of increased revenue. This represents a real aspect of the long-term benefits of improved information management, and while it may be difficult or cumbersome to assess what that opportunity cost is, and its value, a useful proxy is available: the wage cost of an hour of an employee's time, given that (in theory at least) a company pays its staff according to their value.

Importantly, the last example represents a resource saving rather than an input saving. Because the images are created in-house, that in itself is an activity of the company, which is impacted by the change and therefore should be included as an activity in the logic model. There are no real inputs to the activity of photo taking—it is creating something new from no "raw materials," but the resources required to carry out the activity (people's time as well as camera equipment, direct travel costs, and travel time, etc.) do carry a cost.

Other resource savings in this example are realized through faster search for assets, saving time in the asset acquisition and content creation process. If metadata is optimized to include useful rights information, time savings could be realized by legal teams, again creating time for pursuit of new opportunities. As process and technology improvements are made earlier in the information life cycle, more benefits will be realized downstream. There are of course

---

9 It is important to note that if employees need less time to complete a task but this freed-up time is not used for other purposes, there would not be an economic saving.

also resource costs in our example, which represent the "investment" side of the ROI analysis. Some of these, like the purchase of new software, are relatively simple to capture, but one must also account for additional hardware costs, ongoing support costs, and so on.

Additionally, the one-off time costs of rolling out a new system must be captured: from initial installation through end user training, the time required of those involved must be anticipated. Beyond that, time will be required to populate the system with useful assets and metadata. Investments in people and time play critical roles in all manner of IM program transformations, whether or not a purchase of software is involved.

It should also be noted that while the "alternative scenario" begins with initial investment, changes may take time. Major system implementations or process changes are often rolled out to different teams in phases. After rollout, adoption can take time, and new technology and processes usually require a phase of debugging during which the new working methods are erratically applied. Depending on how big an impact this would have on the ROI of a new system, this may need to be considered—returns may not be realized until sometime after the process begins.

Measuring and quantifying outputs and outcomes can be more difficult. In this example, outputs are unlikely to be substantially altered; the activity in question still produces images used on packaging. However, let's say the new system, by making assets more easily searchable, allows for greater reuse of certain assets. This represents a reduction in inputs required to achieve the same outputs and thus is an efficiency improvement, but it could also result in improved outcomes, such as increased revenue, if "better" or "more appropriate" images were used. Measuring this value can be tricky, as can outcome improvements such as risk reduction (e.g., through greater clarity around image rights in the new system) or morale improvements (e.g., if the new system were to reduce confusion around where to find images).

It is sometimes the case that it is not feasible to attempt to measure and/or value these outcomes—while revenue represents a good proxy, it can be difficult to isolate the effect on revenue caused by a new system, given both time lag and the presence of a multitude of other factors affecting revenue. This need not derail the ROI analysis, however. By measuring what is possible to measure (reduction in risk incidents due to improper rights issue, for instance) and simply outlining other outcomes improvements using the logic model structure, the analysis provides greater information, in context, on outcomes improvements that can sit alongside other quantified aspects. This requires more subjective interpretation than a single number but still helps aid the decision maker, which is the real purpose of ROI.

Finally, it is also important to think about the uncertainty of one's ROI estimates. If assumptions have been made or data estimated, it is worthwhile to consider how a change in those data points would affect the ROI results, as well as the potential impact of external events beyond the scope of the analysis.

CONCLUSION

As mentioned above, the purchase of new technology often prompts an exploration into ROI. In this chapter, we have defined what ROI means, explained its applicability to information management, set out a brief overview of a logical structure for breaking down its components, and explained some of the aspects of measurement and validation.

It is easy to understand why the significant financial cost and resulting deep changes to process must be justified with a close examination of the costs and benefits. As touched on above, however, it is just as important to assess ROI before embarking on projects that don't require a direct cash outlay but significantly alter any aspect of IM practices, such as major revisions to a taxonomy or metadata model, changes to workflows, or onboarding of new teams to existing technology and process. Transformative IM projects require investment of time and effort, as well as the sustained attention of those involved. Just as with a direct investment of cash, the return on an investment of people and time must be assessed to clarify the value for all involved. The distinction between financial and economic ROI detailed above should help clarify the difference between "the balance sheet" and value created.

Our overarching aim for this chapter has been to show the value of approaching information management from an economic perspective, to help understand the impact of a new approach in terms of investment (an increase in resources required to set up and support a new system) and its returns, which include both cost savings (a consequent reduction in resources and inputs due to a new system) and improved outputs and outcomes. While concepts of value for money and benefits versus cost are not new, digging into them can seem complex and daunting. However, approaching such a problem armed with a logical framework, exploring the impact of any change, and quantifying it where possible, helps inform decision makers to invest in the most beneficial information management technology and practices for their business.

PART III
Technology and Architecture

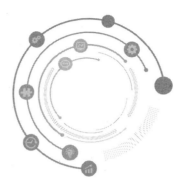

CHAPTER 11

THE CONSUMERIZATION OF ENTERPRISE SOFTWARE

by Robert F. Moss

There was a time when the most sophisticated technology that many people used on a daily basis was what they used at work. And for good reason. Computer hardware was expensive, and even after you bought the computer you had to shell big bucks for applications to run on it. Those applications weren't very versatile or useful for everyday home life, and we had to buy books or take training course to learn how to use them. Few families even had broadband connectivity in their homes. That kind of highfalutin technology was the stuff of the business world.

In the past two decades, though, the emergence of the digital world—and the leaps in consumer technology that made it possible—

has completely reversed the picture. Now, an average office worker (and not just someone in a technical job) carries around in his or her pocket a piece of technology with more memory and processing power than would be found in the largest server in their company's data center twenty years before. And they all know how to use them, too—how to take photos of the kids and email them to their grandparents or how to find a good restaurant in a strange city or book a hotel while sitting in an airport.

These days, the worst digital experience for many of us occurs when we arrive at work; sit down at our desk; and launch the clunky, slow, hard-to-use application that runs the core of our business—and groan while we watch the progress bar and wait for the system to load.

Consumer technology, quite simply, has reset our expectations as technology users. We have grown accustomed to the clean, simple, and efficient user experiences of our smartphones, our tablets, and even our televisions—the technology we purchase ourselves and use ourselves. And, increasingly, we are bringing those same expectations to work.

Let's put it more bluntly: Do our corporate applications really have to be so terrible?

The short answer is that they don't, and increasingly companies are starting to realize that making their applications not be terrible isn't nearly as difficult as many once thought. The key is to "consumerize" our enterprise applications, and the first step to doing that is to embrace digital thinking and user-centric design.

WHAT IS A CONSUMERIZED APPLICATION?

Let's pause for a moment to consider what we mean when we talk about "enterprise applications" and the process of "consumerizing" them.

An enterprise application is, simply, a business application—typically ones designed for a larger company and ones that are specialized to the particular operational processes of that company. Some of these core business systems are similar across many industries—financial and accounting programs, human resources information systems (HRISs), salesforce automation tools. Others are very specific to a particular industry—electronic medical records (EMRs), media asset management (MAM) systems, airline ticketing, and scheduling systems. For our purposes, though, an enterprise application is the opposite of a consumer application—one purchased by businesses for complex business purposes. They are typically more complex, more specialized, and much more expensive than the type of applications used by consumers on their laptops and smartphones.

"Consumerizing" these enterprise applications means updating them so that they share the same characteristics of the consumer applications that have set our user expectations so high in the first place. Here are just a few of those characteristics:

- **Usability**: They must have engaging, intuitive user interfaces that make complex tasks easy to perform. No one goes to a four-hour training class to learn how to use iTunes. Our mantra for consumerizing enterprise applications should be this: *no end user should have to go to a training class to learn how to use our application.*

- **Multimedia**: Consumer apps integrate images and videos and media seamlessly, for twenty-first century users carry around in their pockets a device with a more powerful camera than those used by the top professional photographers and videographers just a few years ago.

- **Best-of-Breed Components and Mashups**: Consumerized apps incorporate the vast array of powerful (and, remarkably, often free) technology that is now at our fingertips. Think text messages, geolocation, maps, voice recognition—how you can click on an address and immediately get directions there from your current location or click on a link and place a phone call without dialing a digit.

- **Being "Cloud Native"**: It's sort of a buzzy term, but the underlying concept is sound. That means: designed and implemented in the cloud first, to be hosted on a virtual cloud-based infrastructure, delivered over the Internet (though probably via secure connection), and consumed in a browser or, alternatively, via a lightweight device-specific app that is delivered and updated seamlessly via the Internet.

- **Openness and Interconnectivity**: An important first step is having a lightweight, easily accessible application programmatic interface (API) that allows an application to be quickly and effectively integrated with other applications. But it means more than that: like users having a profile and identity (e.g., Facebook, Twitter, or maybe just a corporate identify management system) that they can link into and not have to create a separate user profile (and, for Pete's sake, a separate username and password) just to use our application.

- **Responsiveness**: Consumerized apps are responsive in two ways. First, they are fast. Waiting thirty seconds to retrieve a record while a progress bar ticks away isn't sufficient. That record needs to pop right up and pop fast. Second, consumerized apps are responsive to different devices—which is to say, different screen resolutions and interface capabilities. We may be using the application on a desktop from a web browser or connecting on our tablet or pulling it up on our mobile phone, but it shouldn't matter—the application should be responsive to our usage context and allow us to accomplish whatever it is that needs to get done.

- **Near-Real Time**: The digital world can wait a few seconds, even a few minutes, for complex transactions to complete, but three to five business days doesn't cut it. In the digital era, we can hear a song on a TV show, hit Google to find out what it is, bounce over to iTunes and purchase it, and be listening to it in under a minute. There's no having to wait until a batch process runs at night and transfers the information from one system to another or until the song is queued up for shipping and gets delivered to us once someone gets around to filling the order.

- **It Just Works**: Perhaps most important, in today's consumer applications, the incredible complexity of what is occurring behind the scenes is hidden from the user. Users don't want to know—and there's no reason why they should know—all the complicated steps that must occur from the time they heard that catchy song in the background on their favorite TV show until it's playing in their earbuds. It just works.

Okay, that is a lot to ask for. But it's not an impossible request. There's a simple reason why we struggle to achieve these things in the typical enterprise application environment. While the technology available to build applications has changed dramatically in recent years, the way we go about building them hasn't.

In the last decades of the twentieth century, we developed elaborate methodologies and standardized processes for building applications, and we trained our teams and ourselves to follow those practices, learning from hard experience that if we didn't follow those methods we usually got burned.

The way we used to structure our software projects—big design up front, waterfall schedules, copious documentation, and long postdevelopment testing—wasn't wrong. In fact, it was the most reliable way to structure projects and ensure success in a world of expensive, centralized technology, limited interface capabilities, and hierarchical, slow-moving organizations.

But that doesn't mean it's the best way to build applications today.

USER-CENTRIC DIGITAL DESIGN

These days, companies place a lot of emphasis on their consumer experience—on how the external purchasers of our products or the users of our services interact with our company. And that's exactly how it should be. But too often we forget about our own internal users, even though they are key consumers of our enterprise applications and, in fact, have the same needs and expectations as external consumers.

Far too often, when it comes to creating software, we still think of design primarily as interface design—that is, the realm of graphic designers who work at the screen level, taking rough screen ideas (often, wireframes created by business analysts) and making them look nice—colors, fonts, drop shadows, and all that stuff. In effect, we take the old creative services roles from our linear, print-based world and try to shoehorn them into the new digital paradigm.

But that doesn't quite work. Sure, the cosmetic, look-and-feel elements are very important in a digital environment. But, just as our consumer applications are very different today than they were thirty years ago, the role of the designer in the digital age needs to be something quite different, too. Digital designers are not just designing screens. They are designing user experiences—often experiences that exist and interact in both online and offline forms. More than anything else, they need to shepherd a user through the process of completing a specific task, not just provide attractive buttons and widgets for users to twiddle and figure out how to translate into a task.

Let's consider the typical enterprise application today. Regardless of whether it's a commercial product sold by an enterprise software company or a proprietary application created by an internal IT team, there's a high probability that its primary interface mode is going to be tons of tabbed dialogs and drop-down menus. Each of those tabs is cluttered with dozens of data entry fields jammed together along with copious buttons that, when clicked, launch dialog boxes with still more data fields and buttons.

These interfaces are almost uniformly a drab gray with small, boxy fields and tiny font, but the problem is not that they're unattractive. The real problem is that, while they allow the user to access and update all sorts of data, they don't guide them through that task. In fact, users typically need training sessions and help guides just to understand how to manipulate all those controls and get their job done.

Do these instructions sound familiar?

> To set up a new account, first enter the company name, industry, and other general information on the **Main** tab—and don't forget the SIC code. If you aren't sure of the SIC code, click the **Lookup** button, scroll to find the proper industry, and click **Select**.
>
> Next, click on the **Addresses** tab and enter the primary business address, and, if the billing address is different, click the **Add Address** button and add an address of type "billing." Then, click to the **Contacts** tab, click **Add Contact**, and enter in the contact information for the primary billing contact. Now, don't forget that if it's a referral from another customer you need to click on the **Relationships** tab and click **Add Relationship** and choose the type "Referrer" and . . .

That's an awful lot of clicks, and there are any number of things that can be forgotten and go wrong, and, boy, will poor Bill get in trouble if he forgets to enter that referral on the **Relationship** tab and the customer doesn't get their discount, and they'll call the call center and it will take a half-hour of a customer service rep's time just to figure out what went wrong.

There's a simple reason that so many enterprise applications are built this way: they were designed bottom-up from the data model by developers who were largely isolated from the end users and the way they would actually use the system in their daily jobs. Working from detailed specifications created by business analysts, they know customer account records must be stored in the database, they know the name and type of each data field that can be stored, and they know what rules must be enforced to make sure the data is valid—and, in the end, the table and field structure ends up getting barfed out onto the screen in a form with little changed from the technical way in which it's stored in the database. The process the user goes through to enter all that data is not built into the system.

Compare that to the process of registering for an Uber account on a smartphone, a great example of a well-designed consumer experience. The user downloads the app from the app store and clicks on the icon for the first time (no web browser required). Immediately, he or she is taken step by step through the process of signing up for an account. At each step, the app takes advantage of every piece of information and hardware capability that's available within the device to make it as simple as possible for the user to get through the registration process and to get him or her hailing a ride (and sending money to Uber) as soon as possible.

For instance, you need a credit card to use Uber, but you don't have to key in that long, multi-digit number. Instead, you're told to place your credit card on a flat surface, hold your phone over it so the app can take a picture. Then, it uses optical character recognition to read the account number off of the card automatically. It's simple, elegant, and frictionless. It just works.

And that's the key to consumerizing enterprise applications: embracing user-centric design. That is, we shouldn't start out by defining data elements and business rules and functional requirements but rather focus on the user, the context in which he or she is using the application, and what he or she is trying to accomplish. We need to design and build our applications a different way, one that incorporates the collaborative, iterative design approaches that the leading consumer software companies use.

HOW TO GET STARTED

Making the transition to digital design and "consumerized" enterprise applications may seem daunting at first, but there are a few concrete, practical steps that can help you and your teams get started.

Keep It Manageable: Start by selecting one key mission-critical enterprise application, and apply user-centric design principles to rethink and redefine the user experience. Small but tangible improvements gain trust and confidence and will not only boost the confidence of the development team but convince the rest of the organization of the importance of embracing additional consumerization initiatives.

Design Begins before "The Business Requirements": To infuse consumer principles into our applications, it is essential that our teams break out of the current software development paradigm—that linear, waterfall model that goes something like this:

Of course, saying this is nothing new—it's what the practitioners of the Agile Methodology have been preaching since 2001, when the Agile Manifesto was published. But far too many organizations say they are "agile" (or, more frequently, "are moving toward agile") and adopt the trappings of the Agile Methodology—sprints, scrums, cards, burn-down charts—without really engaging with and embracing the fundamental design concepts that underlie agile: iteration and co-creation.

I can't count the number of "agile" corporate projects I've seen that use a modified version where the application is built in sprints but otherwise is shoehorned into traditional write-requirements up front. It goes something like this:

1. Elicit, capture, and get sign-off on written business requirements.

2. Plan development in a series of sprints.

3. Begin developing, testing, and deploying code to a development environment in a series of sprints.

4. Move finished "release 1" of an application to a test environment for "user acceptance testing."

5. Deploy release 1 to production.

This hybrid approach may allow the end users to get a peek at the software during the development phase, but beyond that it gains none of the benefits of agile iterativeness and maintains the stubborn fallacy that we can know all the "business requirements" up front.

Consumer software design is not a linear but an iterative process. The business requirements need to emerge iteratively out of the collaborative design process, through prototyping and early stage development, evolving into a sharper picture as the application develops.

Design Up Front: Do you have a lead designer for your enterprise application initiatives? You should. This applies equally whether you are building a custom application internally or implementing a commercial off-the-shelf application from a software vendor (and, in this day and age, there are only a rare few situations when a company should be building enterprise applications in-house). This sounds counterintuitive when we talk about third-party packages, because isn't that software already designed and built? Why do we need a lead designer to implement it?

Because when we do it right we're not just designing screens, we're designing a system. And we're not just designing a system, we're designing a new business process. In some cases, we may even be designing an entirely new market face for our company and launching a brand-new service offering to the world. And in this new digital world where everything—our enterprise computer systems, our mobile devices, our industrial machinery, our automobiles—are increasingly connected (that much-hyped "Internet of Things"), we're also designing not only how people will use our systems but how other systems will connect with and interact with them.

When does that designer engage? Is it once the requirements are all written and it's time to simply design pretty screens, or is it at the very beginning of the process? Does the designer engage directly with the end users and the key project stakeholders? When we're doing it right, that designer is there from the very beginning.

Don't Reinvent (and Rewrite) the Wheel: This is critical. If we want great experiences, we don't want to waste time writing code to do a function that someone else has already written a thousand times in the past. The best consumer applications embrace this philosophy of reuse.

There was a time (many decades ago now) when software developers still wrote their own databases. No one (fortunately) undertakes to do that. And yet countless internal enterprise applications have custom-built functionality to handle chat and communications, workflow, notifications, alerts, calendars, messaging, maps, and any number of other things that are already commodity products available from any number of sources. Increasingly, there's absolutely no reason to write our own user management, caching, logging—anything that is not specific and unique to our particular application. The very first question our teams should ask is: What third-party (and, preferably, open source) library or component can we use to fulfill that function?

FOCUS ON THE CURRENT STATE (BUT WITH THE PROPER DISTANCE)

I can't remember the number of times I've heard this phrase when kicking off a new business process project: "We don't need to focus on the current state."

I don't think the people saying this are bad people, necessarily. Most of them, in fact, are probably good to their families and rarely steal. They repeat this poor canard for a most understandable reason: the current state we are trying to fix is, generally, downright awful. It wasn't planned, it wasn't designed—it was cobbled together over the course of years out of panicked expediency. It's inconsistent, poorly documented, and rife with manual workarounds and mistakes. The last thing we want to do when designing the future state is to just slap a coat of paint on the current one.

"Let's not pave the cowpaths," such people are wont to say, and I agree with them. We shouldn't just blindly pave cowpaths (or blindly pave anything, for that matter, for that sounds quite dangerous). But we definitely should study those cowpaths and make sure we understand them. Sure, Bessie may have just ambled off that way one day and then kept ambling off that way day after day because that's always the way she off and ambled and she never thought to see if there might be a better route.

But maybe, even though there's a more direct path straight across the plain in front of us, that route has an annoying tendency to flood every few weeks during the summer, wiping away any creature unfortunate enough to find itself there. Or maybe there's a delightful patch of clover just over that hill that we can't see from here but makes for a delicious snack.

The point is this: we need to study the current state not because of the what or the how—things we may not want to carry forward into the future—but rather the why. Why did we decide to do things that way? Seventy percent of the time the answer is simply that we've always done it that way or it seemed like the easiest thing at the time or we had some sort of limitation that we were working around that doesn't exist anymore. But 30 percent of the time there's a really critical reason—our biggest client insists on it, we are required by law in the state of Arkansas to do it, we once had a really big data breach, and this was put in place to address it—and we really need to make sure we account for that situation in our shiny new future state design.

Proximity Matters: Our designers and developers need to sit next to their users. It's really quite incredible how eye opening and illuminating it is to do a chairside—just have your development team members sit next to the actual end users of the software and watch them do their jobs for an hour, or even fifteen minutes. Suddenly everything they are building makes sense because they understand not just what the system needs to do but why it needs to do that and, therefore, how it needs to work.

Ultimately, it's not about aesthetics (though people enjoy using beautiful technology much more than ugly technology), and it's not about making our employees happier (though it's good to have happy employees, which will allow us to retain great people and attract even more). Application usability has a tremendous and immediate effect on employee productivity and operational costs, and we can realize huge savings by eliminating time-consuming manual steps and reducing errors and the associated work of fixing. Even more important, well-designed technology can allow us to win more business, increase revenue, and even move into entirely new lines of business.

Today's enterprise applications are complex, but they don't have to be confusing or hard to use. In fact, they can't be confusing or hard to use for much longer. Our employees and our clients and our key constituents have come to expect a certain level of consumer behavior in their daily use of technology in their personal lives. With a little bit of thoughtful effort, there's no good reason why we can't give it to them in the systems they use at work, too.

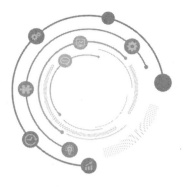

CHAPTER 12

DATA SECURITY

by Jeremy Collins

So far in this book we have given you a solid foundation in the things you need to consider when it comes to transforming, organizing, and communicating your digital architecture and assets.

In this chapter, we give a taste of some important aspects to consider when it comes to securing those assets. It may be tempting to skip over this chapter, thinking that your organization already has this covered or that this is a problem for the IT department. While there is some validity in that assumption, we think it is important that everyone involved in the creation, management, or distribution of information has an awareness of security. During any kind of digital transformation, it is better to consider security as an integral part of that transformation rather than something you bolt on afterward.

A note on terminology: There are many names for digital assets—data, files, documents, images, clips, etc.—so we will use the term *information* to encompass all of these things. Our intention is to provide you with a positive, pragmatic framework for your security context and not to cause you to lose sleep. And in the words of Douglas Adams, "Don't panic"—we won't be asking you to log into a firewall console and configure IP routing tables.

KEY PRINCIPLES

There are three common guiding principles[10] of information security:

1. Confidentiality

2. Integrity

3. Availability

Before we explore these principles, take a moment to consider what each of these words means to you, your work, and your organization. And if, until this moment, you have equated "security" only with "confidentiality" do not worry—you would be in very good company.

As we hope becomes clear, there are several competing tensions between these three facets of security. The balance between these will depend on your business, so while we cannot prescribe a perfect solution, we can at least help you have productive conversations.

---

10 "ISO/IEC 13335-1:2004—Information technology -- Security techniques -- Management of information and communications technology security," ISO.

CONFIDENTIALITY

If we define an asset as something that has value to the organization, then it is clear that controls should be placed on access to information assets. If controls are not in place, or they are insufficient, then the consequences can be embarrassing and costly. Dangers include:

- The company could sustain damage to its reputation.

- It could result in the loss of trust of clients or consumers.

- Competitors could gain an advantage.

- There could be regulatory or legal implications.

Confidentiality is about placing controls on access and disclosure, and generally the implementation of such controls should be left to specialists. However, it is important that you, as a stakeholder in the information assets, are engaged with defining the scope and requirements of these controls. Questions you might ask include:

- Are systems and networks adequately protected from external attack?

- Do system roles and controls mesh with or impede user workflow?

- Do the levels of access correctly reflect organizational structures and responsibilities?

- Can the system correctly separate "write" vs. "read-only" access as appropriate?

- Do controls comply with regulatory or legislative requirements?

- Do controls comply with the organization's policies?

- Are audit trails in place—for example, who accessed what and when? Does someone need access to those audit trails?

- Can the system highlight unusual patterns of behavior by users?

- Can the systems automatically block users from actions that lead to information breaches (for example email attachments containing personal data)?

- Do the systems adequately support remote working without requiring users to work around security controls?

However you refer to it, your organization has, or is part of, a supply chain. You may outsource your payroll, rely on external subject matter experts, or engage with freelance creatives. More and more individuals and organizations are finding benefits in the "gig economy," and our virtual networks are increasingly widespread and complex.

If you are sharing assets with clients, subcontractors, or other third parties, then the considerations of confidentiality go beyond technical security. Consider the following:

- Is there a nondisclosure agreement signed with the third party?

- When were the company's standard contracts last reviewed?

- Are assets protected by trademark or registered copyright (where jurisdiction supports this)?

- Are assets watermarked, or do they have identifying metadata embedded within them?

- Is there an audit trail of what, when, and by whom assets were released?

- Is there a protocol for the secure exchange of information in place or needed? (Email is not secure.)

- Is there an agreed data destruction policy with the third party?

INTEGRITY

Integrity means ensuring that your information is complete, correct, and up to date. While this aspect of information management encompasses governance, workflow, and more than can be covered in the context of security, it is important that controls are placed on how, when, and by whom data can be created, modified, or deleted.

Of course, if your systems are decentralized—for example, exchanging information in manually updated spreadsheet files— then it is almost impossible to guarantee data integrity. In this scenario you may find that too much valuable time is spent in arguments about data quality rather than actually using data for the purpose it was intended. If this sounds familiar, we might suggest that you prioritize the creation of a "sole source of truth" so that your information can become more of an asset than a burden.

Although important, the centralization of information does not in itself guarantee integrity. If we wish to leverage greater collective intelligence ("many eyes") to help us identify potential errors, then we introduce a tension with confidentiality—namely how widely the information is disseminated. And if very tight controls are placed on who can make changes, it may take longer for data integrity issues to be resolved.

Finally, we return to the problem of exchanging information. For example, you may need to communicate some data that has important financial or contractual implications. Within your organization, the recipient will likely have access to the same systems as you, and if you are confident that data integrity controls are in place, then you should be equally confident that the recipient sees the same information. But if the recipient is outside of your organization, how can you both feel guaranteed that you are viewing exactly the same information? One option is to grant them access to your systems, but this may be impractical, costly, or technically unfeasible. A common approach is to convert textual information into a "read-only" format such as PDF, however, for numeric data this can be unwieldy, and anyway, PDFs can be modified. The purpose of this paragraph is to make you aware that there is a technical solution to this problem, called a hash or checksum, which may be appropriate if you need to guarantee the integrity of particularly critical data. In essence, a code is generated from your data, and this code can be exchanged with your recipient. Now, if it is suspected that any part of that data is modified, rather than attempt a laborious or error-prone comparison, creating a checksum will answer the question. Any difference, however minor, will result in a new checksum, which can easily be compared with the original.

AVAILABILITY

Near-perfect confidentiality would mean locking away information assets so tightly that no one could use them. This is most likely not the scenario you are looking for if you are interested in making better use of those assets.

Conversely, maximum availability could mean distributing your data so widely that confidentially is compromised. To use an example, a perfectly valid way of creating off-site backups of your personal digital assets (photographs, home movies, that novel you'll get around to finishing one day) is to periodically copy those files to an external drive and give them to a friend or family member for safe keeping (off-site backups are important to guard against fire and theft). Perhaps you also have spreadsheets of personal finances—do you want to give those to your friend? If you decide to encrypt or password protect those files, then you introduce the risk of forgetting passwords or losing encryption keys, rendering your backups useless.

If you or your organization are using cloud storage (DropBox, OneDrive, Crashplan, etc.) instead of the friend system, then these concerns still apply—How much do you trust that vendor? Where is your data stored? Is it within a legal jurisdiction that protects your rights? What happens if that vendor ceases trading or is acquired by another company? What are their security policies and practices?

Having a good backup scheme is crucial for ensuring availability, and the security of backups is an important consideration, but availability also applies to live data. If your systems are held on one server, you are accepting that there will be some downtime—for planned system maintenance, hardware failures, or malicious denial of service attacks. For a higher level of availability, your systems will need to be replicated across multiple databases, servers, or locations, and so you are increasing the surface area of your risk. Again we see some of the competing tensions between confidentiality, integrity, and availability.

RISK, COST, AND BENEFIT

Implementing security is about mitigating risk. What is your attitude toward risk? More importantly, what is your *organization's* attitude toward risk? It will depend on the industry you are in, your leadership and culture, and external factors such as regulation and competition. Is this written down anywhere or discussed at a leadership level? Your organization's attitude toward risk should help to inform your approach to information security.

When evaluating risk, we might consider the *cost of failure* and the *probability of failure* alongside the *cost of success* and the *value of success*.

Any transformation, digital or otherwise, should have some form of options appraisal at its heart. A good options appraisal will often include the null hypothesis—that the proposed change will have no effect and therefore do nothing.[11] We hope you are not content to do nothing—i.e., ignore security altogether—as the *cost of failure* is too high. If there are regulatory or legal implications to information security breaches, then experts in your particular industry should be able to provide estimates of potential penalties. Legal costs will depend on the jurisdiction and damage caused, but

---

11 For readers well versed in statistics, please forgive this rather loose use of the term.

we think it sufficient to say that these costs will not be trivial. A 2015 study by the Ponemon Institute estimates the average total cost of a data breach at $3.79 million (USD), and while there may be differing views and research as to the cost of data breaches, it is generally agreed that these costs are increasing year on year.

While large organizations often have an uncanny ability to survive reputational damage caused by information breaches, this is not necessarily true for small to medium enterprises—here the cost of failure can be total, and the organization may be forced to cease trading (according to Experian, 60 percent of small companies go out of business within six months of a data breach). Competition damage should not be ignored, either. If you are in the business of creating digital content, then you will be aware of instances where release-quality products have been leaked and a revenue-generating product is forced to compete with an apparently free version of itself.

We are on slightly shakier ground if we attempt to estimate the *probability of failure*. You may find some broad-stroke benchmarks that place your chance of a hack or data breach in any given year at around 10–20 percent. These sound like pretty good odds, and so maybe it is worth taking the risk. Weigh this against the fact that attacks are getting more sophisticated and the cost of failure is getting higher—we recommend that you do not simply accept the risk.

The *cost of success* can usually be quantified with more certainty. Your organization may need to add additional security controls to its systems, which will come with costs associated with hardware, software, advisory services, implementation, and maintenance. As we discussed above, even though your role may not be directly related to IT and security, we strongly encourage you to become involved in these discussions. You have a valuable insight into your information assets and the tensions between the confidentiality, integrity, and availability of those assets, and a security review process would greatly benefit from that insight.

Unfortunately the *value of success* is often (if subconsciously) perceived to be zero. Success is expressed in negatives—we *don't* get hacked or we *don't* have users overwriting our valuable information with garbage.

We do not have to give equal weighting to the cost, probability, and value factors when evaluating risk, and in fact we rarely do. If someone were to offer you ten million dollars to jump off one of the Petronas Towers,[12] we suspect you would politely decline—the cost of failure is too high whatever the value of success. So while we may lack confidence in any estimates for the probability of failure, this uncertainty is outweighed by other factors.

THE HUMAN FACTOR

Information security is not just a technical challenge—there are no black (or beige) boxes you can plug in that will solve all of your problems. The way humans interact with systems and processes must also be considered, and good security is designed with people in mind.

Recall all of those corporate policies that no doubt you have carefully read and committed to memory. Amongst them will be documents with titles such as "IT privacy and security policy," "data protection policy," and "business continuity and disaster recovery." When organizations reach a certain level of perceived maturity, these policies are developed partly in an attempt to mitigate and address some of the human factors in security.

---

12 The left one or the right one or even that bridge bit in the middle—it's up to you.

This may be a good time to take a fresh look at those policies.[13] As you are transforming the digital landscape of your business, are they fit for the purpose? Are the contents of these policies clearly communicated? Just as importantly are the reasons for, and meaning of, these policies communicated? Documented policies are a very good part of a multilayered approach to security, as they clearly define intent and restrictions, and a review of policies should be a recurring agenda item for senior management.

It is very difficult to mitigate against every inept action or against determined corrupt intentions, but you should ensure that all staff and other stakeholders are clearly informed as to their and the organization's responsibilities when handling information assets—particularly if you are dealing with personal information.

---

13 Or if they do not exist, consider creating them.

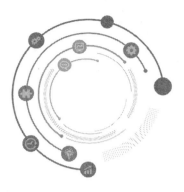

CHAPTER 13

TECHNOLOGY VENDOR SELECTION: GETTING IT RIGHT THE FIRST TIME

by Reid Rousseau

While a technology solution is just one piece of an organization's digital initiative puzzle, it is an integral component in planning for long-term success when facing increasing digital demands. Technology, however, requires a significant front-loaded investment of time, money, and resources to ensure it is successfully utilized in an environment. This starts with the vendor selection process, which can be daunting considering its many complicated moving parts. However, there are right and wrong ways to do it, and the information provided in this chapter aims to provide best practice insight and demonstrate the value of conducting a measured, phased approach, so that the right solution will be selected the first time.

ASKING THE RIGHT QUESTIONS ABOUT TECHNOLOGY AND THE VENDOR MARKET

DEVELOP PROJECT VISION AND CONDUCT CURRENT STATE DISCOVERY

Two main objectives should precede a vendor selection process: defining the project vision and completing current state discovery. Thoroughly completing each objective lays the foundation for a targeted vendor selection process that gets it right the first time. Defining the project vision identifies clear business objectives and goals for future business growth and identifies what a technology solution aims to serve. It is also a prime opportunity to engage users and leadership from all impacted departments to ensure that any technology initiative aligns with enterprise goals. Current state discovery and business analysis should be completed to define project scope, identify business requirements, and inventory information management needs in the current technology landscape.

Developing business requirements is a key step in discovery. This process is an opportunity to:

- document all current state business requirements

- uncover business requirements that may not be visible to leadership

- envision a new future state

- identify user experience (UX) requirements and influencers on user adoption

- engage the IT department to document technical, security, and platform requirements

- assess the required integrations to other internal and external systems and applications

- prioritize requirements for internal and RFP purposes

It is important to consider and include all affected stakeholders in the process to ensure thoroughness of requirements and to build a common understanding of business priorities, project vision, and technology needs. Throughout the vendor selection process, the requirement priorities should be regularly referenced in order to maintain alignment with must-have needs and avoid scope creep. As the selection process proceeds, thorough current state documentation can be an important resource to rely on when considering how market solutions can address an organization's needs. It is the foundation that can guide decision making in identifying best-fit solutions that align with information management, functionality, and business requirement perspectives.

BUILD VENDOR MARKET KNOWLEDGE

Once discovery is complete, the next step is to research the technology vendor market. The market landscape has many players and can often be challenging to navigate. Luckily, there are a variety of vendor research channels to employ, including vendor websites, industry reports, informational vendor outreach, conferences, and partnering with third-party consultancies to execute vendor analysis. The vendor research process should also include industry analysis of technology decisions of similar size organizations and their respective success. Third-party consultancies, industry reports, and outreach can all provide valuable information to complement vendor market-specific research.

When performing vendor research, it is essential to maintain an agnostic perspective and to review vendors based on the level to which they do or do not provide required functionality, while remembering to not be overly influenced by marketing collateral, a flashy interface, or existing vendor relationships. Building knowledge of the vendor marketplace will allow an organization to gain an understanding of solution offerings, develop specific questions for an RFP, and identify a short-list to target in an RFP process.

WHAT TO EXPECT FROM THE RFP PROCESS

RFP DEVELOPMENT

As vendor research wraps up, the organization should begin to draft an RFP for release to vendors. It is critical to compile a clearly organized RFP that addresses all requirements and information requests. Approaching the RFP process as an opportunity for open dialog with vendors that will foster the process's efficiencies, ensuring vendor time is respected and the vendor relationship is off to a positive start.

The RFP should paint a complete picture of your business and technology needs:

- explanation of project goals

- glossary

- business and IT requirements

- requirement priorities

- pricing and total cost of ownership

It is important to carefully develop the RFP and maintain clear communication with the vendors so that the RFP distribution and response process runs efficiently and is completed in a timely manner. One of the vendors will likely become a long-term partner, and establishing a positive relationship from day one can have long-term impact.

ANALYZING RFP RESPONSES

Multiple reviewers should read responses carefully and score them according to quantitative and qualitative analysis. The importance of taking time to thoroughly review each response cannot be overstated. It is an essential part of building a comprehensive understanding of how each system meets requirements, while viewing vendor feedback in the context of the most important functionality and intangible priorities of the organization. Intangible priorities include, but are not limited to, the cultural alignment of the vendor, vendor support structure, user adoption influences, and the vendor's viability and roadmap. While pricing estimates should also be considered at this stage, it should be understood that price estimates could still fluctuate significantly as the process moves forward and the product offering's scope and implementation roadmap are defined.

Once evaluations are performed through a weighted scoring methodology, the project team should be able to identify one to three candidates to invite for system demonstrations, ideally to be performed live on site. A group consensus for the vendors selected to proceed is key so that all stakeholders are in agreement that the right selection decisions are made at each step of the process.

WHAT TO EXPECT FROM SYSTEM DEMOS

System demos are a critical opportunity for a vendor to show the "how" of its technology's functionality. Often a critical factor in a system's fit is not if it provides a feature requirement but *how* that feature works and performs its functionality—is it intuitive and easy to use? Will it require workflow redesign to implement, or can it be slid into existing process flows? To get the most out of demos and to ensure a vendor provides genuine exposure to their product, it is worth investing time and planning to define their scope by creating a demo script and use cases for a vendor to design. Developing scoping documents for vendors ensures demonstrations will be efficient and that information presented addresses organizational priorities and establishes parity between presentations for the sake of easier "apples to apples" evaluation.

It's important to compile all relevant information from demonstrations for consideration in the final selection decision process. Once demonstrations are complete, collect collateral from the vendor presentations and demo recordings for additional reference as needed, and coordinate with vendors to confirm any action items coming out of the demos (follow-up questions, additional information requests). Depending on demo outcomes, it may be valuable to request that vendors provide a test license to the system for an organization to pilot for a short period of time.

MAKING A FINAL DECISION

Initial demo feedback should be discussed on completion of each demo to capture immediate impressions. If an organization is able to pilot a system, the time spent during the trial period can be dually spent compiling, scoring, and analyzing demo outcomes and preparing for final decision making.

After the rigorous efforts of a vendor selection process, coming to a final decision of a single solution can be challenging. Discussions about solutions have the potential to become strongly polarized or even stalled if stakeholders become attached to a particular solution or develop cold feet in having to commit to a particular system. Organizations must remember that there is rarely a magic bullet solution that will fulfill all requirements at 100 percent. Organizations should maintain a clear record of vendor scores as well as a realistic sense of deal breakers versus areas in which compromises can be made. This allows conversations to remain productive and enables facilitators to approach disagreements rationally, accounting for multiple points of view.

Making a final decision may feel daunting, but a well-managed selection process will help ensure stakeholders develop excitement for the new technology solution and improved future state.

CONCLUSION

Making the right technology decisions the first time involves careful planning and stakeholder engagement. Technology is a significant investment, and the decision will play an impactful role in an organization's enterprise digital strategy. Thus, it is imperative to follow a thoughtful methodology to identify the best-fit vendor and long-term partner to buttress organizational success. The process can be complex and requires strong analysis, communication, and decision-making skills. The methodology discussed in this chapter provides a foundation for a successful vendor selection, emphasizing a measured approach to building organizational knowledge, alignment, and collaboration to reach a consensus on a technology solution.

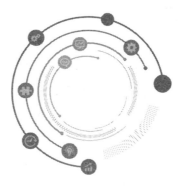

CHAPTER 14

MITIGATING THE PAIN OF LEGACY SYSTEM INTEGRATION

by Jesse Celso

How familiar does this sound: an organization purchases the Ferrari of a certain technology only to have it perform like a go-cart after implementation. More times than not this is due to limitations resulting from integration with existing legacy systems, rather than functionality of the product itself. Whether implementing a new DAM, rights management system, content management system, or workflow orchestration tool, the performance and expected results of the shiny new technology is directly correlated to its ability to effectively communicate with existing legacy systems within a technology ecosystem.

PROBLEM STATEMENT / BUSINESS CASE

In today's world of continuously advancing technology solutions, organizations are often faced with the challenges of integrating legacy systems (outdated applications/systems/technology). It is a reality that all technologists must face. Most organizations do not have the luxury of regularly overhauling their enterprise architecture to keep up with changing technologies, and sometimes that means new system functionality is impacted by integrations with dated systems.

COMMON PAIN POINTS

The pain points commonly experienced in legacy system integrations can be devastating to efficiency and limit the ability to meet the business needs. Some examples are:

- **Dirty Data**—Many legacy systems have a large quantity of data that is inaccurate or inconsistent across applications. Over time, data entry standards may have changed or were never enacted, resulting in poor data quality. Dirty data significantly impacts workflow management, reporting, and user search.

- **Ineffective Search**—If there is inconsistent data across applications and/or lack of integration between systems housing similar data, federation of search across said systems becomes very challenging. The absence of federated search can result in users needing to search in multiple places or even recreate files/data when they are unable to find what they are looking for, resulting in data redundancy.

- **Data and File Redundancy**—Duplicate data and duplicate files will directly impact an organization's bottom line, introducing unnecessary storage costs and time loss due to ineffective user search. Redundancy can also introduce compliance risk, as with more versions comes increased chance of using the wrong content or record.

- **Multiple/Complex Integrations**—In the absence of a middleware or an Enterprise Service Bus (ESB), point-to-point integrations result. This type of integration can lead to a "spaghetti effect," where multiple systems communicate in an unordered manner. This inhibits establishing federated search as well as any type of end-to-end workflow management/monitoring.

KEY CONSIDERATIONS

One of the best ways to mitigate the pain of legacy system integration is the selection of the product that most closely matches the defined evaluation criteria ("best-fit" product). There are some key considerations prior to purchasing your new technology and deciding on approaches to mitigating integration challenges.

- **Business Need**—*What are the needs I am really trying to meet?* It is important to keep a focus on your critical needs rather than getting wrapped up in all the bells and whistles the various sales reps are boasting. In some cases, the best solution is not the most complex or robust but rather has specific functionality that performs very well.

- **Data Complexity**—*How complex is my data?* Perhaps you have thousands of titles, with numerous points of data origination, requiring elaborate data hierarchies. Or perhaps your metadata model is extremely elaborate to meet your content distribution and reporting needs. The complexity of your data is a key factor in selecting the right product.

- **IT Philosophy/Integration Methodology**—*How does my organization approach implementation and enterprise architecture?* Whether your organization adheres to service-oriented architecture (SOA) methodologies or is more simplistic with point-to-point integration, this is a key consideration of how complex your solution should be. For example, it may be critical for an individual solution to have robust workflow management capabilities if an enterprise workflow management tool is not in place.

- **Culture**—*How do our core user groups interact? Are they highly collaborate or mostly work in silos?* Company culture is rarely something that is considered in the decision to implement new technology or deciding which solution is a "best fit," however, the people and dynamics of who will be using the system should always be top of mind.

- **Cost**—*Is budget the key driver for selection?* The decision of which product to purchase often comes down to budget rather than product superiority, making it all the more critical to focus on the core business needs. Another key driver is ongoing maintenance and support costs, which can directly impact budget allocated to other integrated systems.

- **Timing**—*Is technology in the industry about to change?* Considering the maturity of the technology itself is critical, as shifts in technology within your industry can quickly make your newly purchased technology obsolete.

- **Vendor Comparison and Evaluation**—*How do the top vendors stack up against my requirements?* Many organizations do not fully understand how to effectively measure how well a product meets their requirements. Vendor evaluation methodology is critical, as some products may be overkill, and some may have a beautiful user interface but not truly meet the business requirements.

- **The Power of the POC**—Today it is very commonplace to enter into a proof-of-concept (POC) agreement with one or two vendors to demonstrate a product's effectiveness within your own organization. This means that you can actually engage a vendor to prove their solution by scoping a mini project with limited integration and utilizing your own data to test the product's functionality, user acceptance, etc. Most technology vendors are willing to conduct a POC, and it is an excellent way to ensure selection of the "best fit" technology for your organization.

PROPOSED SOLUTIONS

It is important to consider *people* and *process* implications alongside technology—simply adding a new technology solution to the mix likely will not yield the desired results. Some advantageous ways of mitigating the pain points associated with legacy system integrations include:

ENTERPRISE ARCHITECTURE AND TECHNOLOGY

- **Enterprise Service Bus (ESB)/Middleware and Service-Oriented Architecture (SOA)**—Many organizations choose to incorporate an ESB or middleware to create what is known as the "hub and spoke model." This allows an organization to disconnect an old system and integrate its replacement in a simple manner, limiting impact on other systems and workflows managed by the technical ecosystem. Although an ESB or middleware solution can be an expensive implementation initially, savings in future integration costs typically make up for it. This model also allows for a higher level of control and monitoring over messaging and data flow. Service-oriented architecture (SOA) is a methodology that extracts specific functionality from individual systems and presents users with a suite of services. This model is incredibly powerful in ensuring a seamless user experience.

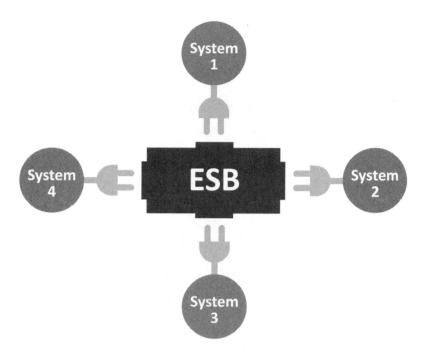

- **Integration Standards**—In recent years, more and more associations composed of system engineers and vendors are being established, for the sake of partnering across the aisle to define integration standards. Standardization makes integrating new systems simpler and aligns it within service-oriented architecture methodology. Vendors are becoming increasingly compliant with these standards, as they recognize its value to their customers. These integration standards include standardized APIs, message structures, and object models, facilitating easier "plug-and-play" integration. One example of such an association is Framework for Interoperable Media Services (FIMS), a self-proclaimed "task force" managed jointly by Advanced Media Workflow Association (AMWA) and European Broadcasters Union. FIMS aims to create flexible, cost-effective solutions to help facilitate seamless future integrations for the benefit of the industry, with no cost of adoption.

- **Master Data Management Tool (MDM)**—Enterprise data management can be incredibly complex, and poor data management will directly or indirectly impact the performance of every system in a technology ecosystem. Depending on the complexity of an organization's data and the number of systems in the ecosystem, implementation of an MDM may be the solution for allowing teams to extract data from legacy systems and provide a single source of data truth for new technology to consume. Many organizations have multiple unique identifiers generated for the same asset. For example, your digital asset management system (DAM) assigns a UID to a piece of content, and your rights management system assigns a UID to a title. The MDM can provide the linking and consolidation of UIDs through business logic, enabling you to have a holistic view of all relevant data for a particular asset's performance.

- **Metadata Management Tool**—Some organizations do not have the need or budget to implement a master data management tool (MDM), and so utilizing a metadata management tool can provide an alternative, less costly yet effective way to provide a clean source of data for new technology. Metadata management tools are lighter weight data management tools, typically with a focus on content-specific metadata rather than enterprise master data management. Think of this tool as a metadata washing machine, consuming metadata from legacy systems and stitching it into a clean metadata model for consumption by other systems. Metadata management tools also provide data stewardship functionality and error reporting, which can be useful in cleaning up source system databases. Similarly to an MDM, metadata management tools can be leveraged for unique identifier management across systems for tracking and reporting at the asset level but on a smaller scale.

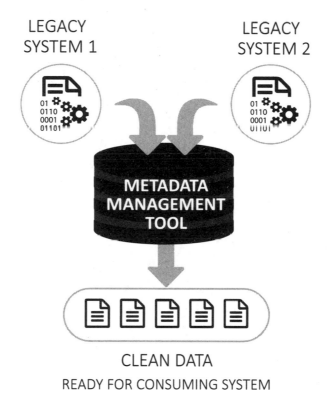

LEGACY SYSTEM 1

LEGACY SYSTEM 2

METADATA MANAGEMENT TOOL

CLEAN DATA
READY FOR CONSUMING SYSTEM

- **Enterprise Search Tool**—Most organizations have numerous sources of data within the enterprise, and this can present challenges in searching for content and information, particularly in point-to-point integration scenarios. Consequently, users may be required to search in multiple places, reducing efficiency and in some cases yielding poor to no results. An enterprise search tool scans all source system databases against which it's integrated and serves search results through a single, central user interface (UI). The more sophisticated solutions allow organizations to customize the search parameters, maximizing search effectiveness per each source system or even the user's business unit.

- **Enterprise Data Mapping**—It is common that separate data models are maintained by each unique technology system. Consequently, there may be fundamental differences in how information is recorded and structured from system to system. For example, a rights management system could utilize the format *Episode_01*, while a digital asset management system could utilize the format *EP-01*. This minor difference can have a monumental impact on integration between the two systems if not mapped correctly. Conducting analysis, documenting detailed field mappings between systems, and defining a controlled vocabulary for representing information formats before a new technology implementation will greatly simplify the integration.

- **Data Stewardship and Governance**—Regardless of the technology system implemented, ongoing data stewardship and governance is critical. The value of technology tools will be minimal without the support of defined data governance processes and dedicated resources accountable for its enforcement. Data will change over the course of its lifespan, evolving with business and industry practices. This makes ongoing data stewardship critical to maintaining data integrity. By establishing data governance and an escalation process for any data issues, data stewards will be empowered to meet challenges on an ongoing basis, resulting in better data quality overall. High-quality data and established data management standards are critical for any successful system implementation.

CONCLUSION

Although the challenges associated with legacy system integration can be monumental, by selecting the "best-fit" technology and having the right processes, methodologies, and technological tools in place, organizations are able to reduce the impact to performance of any new systems added to their technical ecosystem.

PART IV

Archives and Records Management

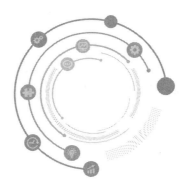

CHAPTER 15

REVOLUTIONIZING THE EXPERIENCE OF AGING CONTENT: THE VALUE OF A QUALITY ARCHIVING PROGRAM

by Mindy Carner

Among the more underrepresented elements of a proper and thorough information management program is the archive. Often treated more as a dumping ground to throw away old documents that are no longer in use, the curated archive can be a useful business tool for improving the discoverability of company content. The value of a properly curated archive cannot be over-stated. The archive stores institutional knowledge and memory of the company. It protects against the dangers of constantly changing digital formats and content ownership and provides an opportunity to repurpose and repackage historical artifacts for marketing and branding efforts or trigger new ideas in an organization.

ARCHIVING KNOWLEDGE

One complaint that many organizations have, and that can cause an endless cycle of knowledge management "reboots," is the continual loss of institutional knowledge through turnover of employees and staff retirement. While a knowledge management structure is a vital element of a company's information management program, it is frequently mistaken for the endgame of institutional knowledge; that is, the content in a knowledge repository needs to change and evolve with the business, while the archive is the final destination for those knowledge assets that eventually lose their value as a template but are still valuable for their historical content. But digital formats change; logos, templates, and designs evolve; and companies go through process transformations, and when these changes occur, an organization loses value from a knowledge base full of outdated content. A knowledge management program requires constant upkeep and conversion to the most sophisticated templates and guides, always maintaining the latest format.

This is a moment where the archive plays a key role by housing older knowledge artifacts that provide value in documenting where the company has been and how the organization has evolved over time. For example, a company may look back at old branding guides, organizational frameworks, historical reports, and various other outputs that speak to how the company operated in the past. Furthermore, it is common for teams to review their past work and achievements as a basis for their strategy and planning for future business cycles. Therefore, capturing this wealth of information is an invaluable process. Beyond just templates and guides that change over time, the actual knowledge and information artifacts themselves have a permanent home in the archive and can be referenced at any time. This provides a gateway for immediate access to historical content only when needed and prevents repositories that are used for day-to-day tasks from filling up.

THE SYSTEM OF RECORD

An archive requires a system of record. This can be as simple as "finding aids"—from the classic physical archive—that literally guide users in finding their content based on medium, topic, or person related. It may also be as complex as a technology solution that houses the metadata about the various artifacts inside the system. For digital artifacts, this type of system would be required to store the various documents, presentations, images, videos, and other creative files, along with their records.

A system of record can offer so much more than just storage and retrieval. A properly designed system can set up automated workflows to streamline new content to archivists for approval or dismissal. It can democratize the use of artifacts while keeping restricted content away from general users. Proper permissions, controls, and group designations can ensure ongoing security around various artifacts, even carrying over existing security levels from integrated systems.

The archive system of record also acts as the single source of truth for all inactive assets. This means that only final versions will be stored in this curated system, which prevents confusion when identifying the correct final version, a problem that can occur in shared drives and document management systems that do not clearly outline the versioning process.

DISCOVERY

An archive facilitates discovery. As users browse for content, they "stumble upon" artifacts that may spark an idea, provide an insight, or answer a question that wasn't yet being asked. Serendipity is as undervalued as archives themselves, and that is equally unfortunate, for these are the moments when innovation happens. The discovery of inspiring historical content can increase the return on investment for projects by sparking new conversations and offering an existing set of content to work with rather than having to start from scratch.

REDUCED RISK OF LOST CONTENT

A curated archive protects an organization from many dangers that it may not have previously considered or anticipated. For example, the constantly changing landscape of digital formats poses a very real threat to the ability to hold on to company knowledge. Imagine the volume of content that has been lost due to the obsoletion of the floppy disc. Discs full of information were discarded once computers started to be released without floppy disc drives. Not only is this physical format now archaic, but also the digital formats of the content may no longer be supported by today's software.

The same goes for video and audio formats. Most audio players cannot support the recordings on formats that have not been updated, rendering that audio useless. Identifying moments when new formats are introduced (and become established in the market), while old formats are still supported to transition content is the difference between well-maintained institutional knowledge and lost content.

RECORDS MANAGEMENT

One component of archiving that can provide lasting value to the organization is the records management program. Deeply intertwined with the archive program, this set of rules and timetables ensures that information goes where it should go, when it should go there—whether that final destination is long-term preservation in the archives or destruction. But records management stops shortly after designating the life cycle of a record. Once a document has been deemed inactive by its retention schedule, it is up to the archive to ensure that, over time, it does not lose value by becoming obsolete, unfindable, or damaged beyond repair.

Records management does the important job of determining the record life cycle. All records have an active life and an inactive life. It is once records reach their inactive life that they are truly at risk. In a moment of shortsightedness, users might feel compelled to free up their disc space by deleting documents that are more than five years old. But a records retention schedule will outline exact details of when an artifact becomes truly inactive and where it should go when it becomes so.

As discussed in detail in chapter 16, managing historical records allows a company to respond with confidence when any litigation requests might arise, foregoing potentially costly searches through data or physical record warehouses. The archive serves as the home for any content deemed valuable for the long term.

PHYSICAL AND DIGITAL ARCHIVAL CONTENT

This book is about the transformation of digital content into insights, innovation, and empowerment. With the archive component of that practice, it may start with transferring content into a digital format. Storage of digital content is cheap and getting cheaper. Aside from certain historical records that must remain in physical format for legal, historical, or aesthetic purposes, converting physical records to digital format for long-term storage may improve discoverability. For instance, finding a record in a digital archive can be an exponentially faster process than finding it in an offsite paper storage facility with questionable labeling and content indexing. Secondly, digitized content that has been treated with ocular character recognition (OCR) is immediately indexable and searchable.

SETTING UP THE ARCHIVE

Most corporate archives will have a physical component. Whether it is a large amount of paper documents, or hundreds of physical ephemera, a physical space will be required, as well as a way to create records and digital surrogates in the archival system of record (SOR). This requires more planning and effort than a digital archive alone, and the metadata around these different formats must be captured. For this reason, the bulk of the effort to set up a corporate archive program will be capturing the correct metadata, understanding the content life cycle—including coordinating with the retention schedules in your records management program—and setting up a training and change management program to ensure that people understand the importance of this work as they go through their content. Once this has been established, regular maintenance will allow the archive to remain relevant and up to date.

Setting up an archive program starts in the same manner as any other information management project: getting executive sponsorship and buy-in. It can be difficult to acquire funds to set up a physical space, acquire a system of record, and get expertise to capture the metadata and workflows around the artifacts, so having a stakeholder who understands the value of saving the company's history and has the power to initiate these changes is key to a successful project. See chapter 18 (Stakeholder Management) for a more thorough discussion of how to accomplish this.

Once sponsorship has been acquired and the project has begun, the first thing to think about is the business requirements for the archive and its system of record. In most cases these will include:

- artifact metadata

- artifact life cycles (for submission workflows)

- program and system governance

- training and change management

Each of these topics is covered as a separate chapter in this book. The process is generally the same for an archive-specific project, with the caveats that artifact life cycles may be influenced heavily by existing retention policies. If policies do not exist for any or all artifacts, then a joint effort with the records management team will fill the gaps. Additionally, archival metadata capture is a practice unto itself. While there will be specific metadata field values unique to the company, archiving is a well-defined practice that captures a set of information about artifacts. These established principles of archival theory should be followed when setting up the archival metadata. Fortunately, these theories are well documented and freely available from the Society of American Archivists.

ARCHIVAL STANDARDS

Describing Archives: A Content Standard is regularly reviewed by field professionals and updated as needed to ensure that the utmost important details about archival artifacts are captured, allowing for their successful findability and use for posterity. Along with this outline of fields to include in the metadata model, the Society of American Archivists has also outlined a freely accessible standard for encoding archival metadata into XML called Encoded Archival Description (EAD), which makes the content machine-readable.

Because archiving is a practice with roots so deeply interlaced with library science, there are many standards that can be readily utilized to improve and streamline the development of metadata for digital artifacts. IPTC and EXIF standards, for example, are embedded into digital images and capture important copyright, date/time, and format details, among myriad others. Incorporating these standards into the archive's final metadata fields is an out-of-the-box capability of many systems-of-record (SOR) technologies.

Another important capability of many SORs is storing high-definition original versions of an artifact that can be reformatted, ad hoc, into web-ready, specifically sized, or otherwise lower resolution derivatives. This allows for a smaller storage size by avoiding saving various versions of the same artifact in the system. In the event that the chosen SOR does not support instant derivative creation, it will be important to learn the difference between lossy compression and lossless compression before making changes to content.

APPRAISAL

A final detail to keep in mind before starting an archive project is to understand the ongoing value of each item. Remember that in some cases, physical items might be saved, taking up expensive storage space (physical artifacts require temperature control and high security), emphasizing the need to whittle out anything that will not provide valuable historical insight. For digital content, the old "garbage in, garbage out" adage applies. Filling up the search index with content that is not useful and will not be viewed will only do damage to the user experience of the system. This makes it all the more important for the system to be curated.

CONCLUSION

An archive project has many elements in common with other information management practices; it necessitates strong metadata to ensure usability of the system and findability of the content. It requires executive buy-in to guarantee that funding can be acquired. And it requires a behavioral change throughout the organization to protect all of the hard work from falling on the wayside. The value of your company's historical artifacts can go well beyond academic interest. The trends in social media, marketing, and advertising to harken back to another age, and/or drum up nostalgia, are continually growing—think "throwback Thursday." The security, also, has incredible implications for avoiding litigation complications, safeguarding important records, and providing a source of truth that can always be referenced. In other words, an archive provides a final and invaluable component of a successful information management program.

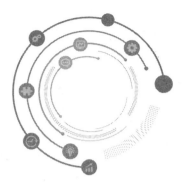

CHAPTER 16

WHY REINVENT THE WHEEL? APPLYING RECORD KEEPING BEST PRACTICES TO DIGITAL STRATEGY

by Gretchen Nadasky

Once assets have been identified, user requirements have been mapped, metadata schemas have been developed, and technology has been chosen, it is time to start thinking about the future. The only thing we know about the future, of course, is that things will change. Digital information is created, received, copied, transformed, and referenced in very short cycles. As an organization grows, the production of information and assets accelerates, generating ever more files, folders, and storage volume. In the past, the growth of information would be obvious by the material piling up in offices, file cabinets, and storage rooms. Eventually, the mess would start to affect productivity and require cleanup and records management. Today, information grows exponentially but hidden from sight within servers or in the cloud. Without visibility, digital chaos can grow unabated for some time and affect productivity in the same way paper would. Using the disciplines of records management, organizations can integrate strategies to control electronic files and maintain efficiency, lower cost, and maintain the RIM structure to protect their critical information.

Records and information management (RIM) addresses the organizing, maintaining, and managing of historical information. RIM protocols are used to make sure paper and electronic evidence of transactions are properly maintained and stored for legal, regulatory, and business needs once they have become inactive. Information that is in the process of being created and consumed is "active," but later it is considered "inactive." Companies often struggle with how inactive information should be held in the event it is required for litigation discovery, regulatory audit, or even just reference several years into the future. In the past, institutional knowledge was held by long-standing employees. Today's fast pace of business transformation constantly displaces people, increasing the need for strong information policies. Information creators may leave the organization, but the responsibility for maintaining the document remains with the company. Organizations that have been in existence for more than a few years typically have exponentially more inactive digital assets than active ones—records management helps to address the problems associated with "old stuff."

ARMA International is the professional association that represents RIM; it also publishes guidelines and educational materials on information governance. One of the main tools for records managers is the Generally Accepted Recordkeeping Principles® ("the Principles"). While the intention of the Principles is to govern officially designated corporate records, the philosophy behind them can be applied to managing inactive creative assets like artwork and video or large caches of data.

CASE STUDY: IMPLEMENTING ENTERPRISE RECORDS MANAGEMENT AT A TV NETWORK

Highly regulated companies generally have mature records management programs to comply with certain laws or rules. Financial, energy, and health-care organizations, for example, report regularly to governing bodies and must be able to produce records quickly. Unregulated companies and private companies sometimes neglect to manage their records because they are not required to do so by an outside regulator or investor.

One privately held television network, subject only to business regulations and tax-reporting requirements, decided to get control over their enterprise information. The company had grown quickly over its twenty-year history to over a thousand employees, storing and producing an overwhelming amount of content that was expensive and complex to manage. In addition, international expansion to geographies where the rules for exchanging information are more stringent than in the United States forced them to reconsider the treatment of certain information, like personally identifiable information (PII).

The company used the disciplines of records management to identify official corporate records that needed to be held for legal or financial reasons but also to identify and control the growth of creative assets. The creative assets included artwork, marketing material, photographs, web-based campaigns, original scripts, pro-motional clips, and long-form video and outtakes. A separate initia-tive for managing original and licensed music was also undertaken.

As a result of using records management practices on all digital and paper assets, the company was able to identify and locate corporate records, monetize hidden creative assets, reduce volumes and storage costs, and increase the efficiency of information in all twenty departments. In addition, they also protected themselves from large legal discovery costs in the event of a large litigation.

PUTTING THE PRINCIPLES INTO ACTION

As authored by ARMA, the Principles consist of eight standards that the management of records should aspire to. They are:

- the Principle of Accountability

- the Principle of Transparency

- the Principle of Integrity

- the Principle of Protection

- the Principle of Compliance

- the Principle of Availability

- the Principle of Retention

- the Principle of Disposition

Sometimes people use the acronym "A TIP CARD" to remember all eight. A corporate records and information management (RIM) policy might refer to these values as part of its guidelines. A digital strategy can use the Principles as a framework to design a program to fit the needs of the organization while also upholding best practices for all facets of information management.

USING THE PRINCIPLE OF ACCOUNTABILITY TO MAINTAIN CONTROL

Accountability means that someone within the organization has been given the responsibility of overseeing how information is handled once it has become inactive. Even in today's world of advanced technology, information doesn't organize itself. Maintaining control can be the responsibility of a designated records manager or can be handled by RIM stewards across the organization. Ideally, to uphold the principle of accountability, there is a person or group of people who make sure that redundant, obsolete, or transient (ROT) information is not building up within the storage systems.

USING THE PRINCIPLE OF TRANSPARENCY FOR AUTHORITY

A digital strategy is only useful when it is understood and supported by all asset creators and consumers in the organization. Communicating rules around how assets must be organized and stored not only prevents chaos down the road but also improves the reputation of the information itself. Communication and training is crucial for a digital strategy to be transparent to all stakeholders. Concise corporate policies also increase the confidence of external parties with relationships to the organization.

USING THE PRINCIPLE OF INTEGRITY TO CREATE "SINGLE SOURCE OF TRUTH"

Integrity of information means it can be trusted as authentic and current. If information is allowed to multiply without control and management via metadata and modeling, then version control is lost and the value of the asset declines. When assets are allowed to move freely, the chain of custody can be lost, undermining trust that the information is original. By establishing rules around originality and custodianship, or document ownership, assets can be relied on as the "single source of truth."

USING THE PRINCIPLE OF PROTECTION TO ENHANCE ENTERPRISE VALUE

In the information economy, the value of digital assets represents the intellectual property of many organizations. Cybersecurity and even physical safety protocols are essential for preserving the valuable information and creative assets produced by employees on a daily basis. Including long-term plans for securing digital assets, even when they have become inactive, must be a key part of the digital strategy to protect the overall value of the organization.

USING THE PRINCIPLE OF AVAILABILITY TO PROMOTE THE USE OF METADATA

In study after study, it has been shown employees spend hours out of their workweek searching for information. In fact, the most efficient way to guarantee information and digital assets will be available is to add metadata. However, there is a misperception that the time it takes to include metadata is not worth the investment. Making availability a priority of the digital strategy will focus users on the benefits of metadata to overall productivity.

USING THE PRINCIPLE OF RETENTION TO CHANGE A "KEEP EVERYTHING FOREVER" CULTURE

In many organizations, people don't think about what happens to information when they are finished with it, or they feel like they will get in trouble if they don't retain everything they have ever created. The principle of retention introduces the idea that information needs to be kept for a period of time but maybe not indefinitely. Retention codes are used in records management to denote the length of time a document must be maintained. As part of the digital strategy, retention codes, published in a retention schedule, describe the length of time records must be held. Changing a culture from "keep everything forever" to responsible retention can lower storage costs and increase efficiency by decreasing ROT while also assuring that important information is held for as long as necessary.

USING THE PRINCIPLE OF DISPOSITION TO EMPOWER EMPLOYEES AND PROTECT THE FIRM

When people think of disposing of records, they sometimes conjure the image of people frantically shoving paper into a shredder—but that image is the opposite of defensible disposition. Defensible disposition means records that have expired or exceeded the required period in the retention schedule are disposed of properly in the course of business. When official electronic records are expunged because they have expired, the action is logged with a certificate of destruction. The process of destruction follows corporate policy and is approved by legal to be sure there is not expectation of legal action on those records. Developing an automated process allows for the disposition of expired information and takes the responsibility out of the hands of employees and places it on the higher authority of the organization that owns the information.

The Principles are an excellent framework from which to develop a digital strategy for inactive records. It is absolutely crucial to consider the implications of not controlling the growth of digital information and take action before it gets out of hand. Digital asset managers don't need to invent a new way of tackling the problem but instead can apply the proven methods of records management creatively to any asset.

CASE STUDY: GLOBAL SPORTS CONTENT MEDIA NETWORK

INFORM – PROBLEM STATEMENT: DAM ASSESSMENT

The client is a globally known and respected media network, offering a comprehensive range of sports media content across television, radio, publishing, web and social media channels. The creative services marketing department is responsible for the creation, distribution, and storage of promotional and marketing content across the enterprise. The highly skilled group has recognized the benefits of an omnichannel approach to the people, processes, and technologies that support the creation and distribution of marketing content. Despite its successes, the department's history of roadblocks has hindered the evolution of its digital asset management (DAM) program. As a result, suboptimal digital asset management has become the norm, and the department relies on substituting a plethora of shared drives and other technologies in place of a true DAM system that could act as a "single source of truth" for creative assets.

TRANSFORM – STRATEGY, SOLUTION, AND BENEFITS

The department leadership were aware of the different pain-points the team faced while performing everyday tasks and responsibilities. To reassess their technology, strategy, and DAM program evolution, departmental leadership engaged Optimity Advisors to perform a rapid review and assessment of current state digital asset operations and to provide improvement opportunity recommendations and an accompanying roadmap of the tactical and strategic next steps to take to thoughtfully evolve the DAM program. Optimity conducted current state system audits and discovery interviews with key stakeholder groups to identify major asset collections, inventory current technology, assess metadata in use, and document DAM requirements.

ASSET COLLECTION INVENTORY

The asset collection inventory documented high-level asset categories and provides accompanying information from descriptive, technical, workflow, and accessibility perspectives. A comprehensive documentation of assets is required before designing a metadata strategy that reflects the asset inventory and supports asset categorization and discovery for end users. The inventory is also a critical reference document to be able to scope, design, select, and deploy technology systems that will appropriately manage assets and evolve in alignment with ever-changing business needs.

TECHNOLOGY TOOL LANDSCAPE

The DAM Technology Tool Landscape Matrix documented the current technologies and tools in use for managing digital asset creation, storage, and distribution. The matrix provides an overview of each system's purpose, identifies departmental and asset touch points, and assigns rankings on how well each system facilitates digital asset management and file transfer. These ratings are then used to determine which systems will or will not be replaced by the DAM.

CURRENT STATE METADATA

To begin work toward a future-state metadata and taxonomy model, the current-state metadata was organized into descriptive, administrative, and technical groupings. The source and repositories were also identified, along with a flag indicating whether or not the field was redundant. This represented a launching point to begin developing a holistic future state metadata model, which will represent the foundation of creative services' digital strategy and provides initial recommendations on which fields to consider for future use.

BUSINESS REQUIREMENTS

Optimity surfaced high-level DAM requirements from stakeholder discovery interviews, aligned and supplemented requirements with industry best practice, and assigned initial priorities to each. This list will be leveraged to guide and expedite the vendor RFP and selection process to ensure potential solutions are assessed according to the client's DAM needs. The above discovery findings then fed into the DAM Maturity Model, which provided a 1–5 maturity ranking of the department's DAM program across fifteen dimensions in four categories and provided the backing for strategic recommendations moving forward. Based on the discovery and DAM maturity rankings, Optimity developed a phased roadmap that included both tactical, near-term and longer term strategic next steps to continue the momentum created by the rapid discovery and assessment. As a result of these efforts, the DAM program was reinvigorated and left the team well positioned to embark on the next phase.

Organizations creating a DAM business case typically consider the positive business impacts (e.g. time saved while working), technology expenditure, time and resources required for implementation, and risks mitigated. Although each of these outcomes are valuable to consider, the quantitative benefit of such a system can often be opaque, thus Optimity has developed a proprietary approach grounded in economic analysis to help reveal the bottom-line value of this investment.

OUTPERFORM

This engagement accomplished two key goals: perform the rapid discovery work required to jumpstart a DAM program and begin communicating strong evidence backing DAM program evolution and a potential technology investment to key executive stakeholders. Optimity's current state discovery documentation and argument for an ROI approach to developing a business case helped the client create and sustain momentum to progress in completing the forthcoming steps and investments that will foster an optimal digital asset management ecosystem.

PART V
Socialization

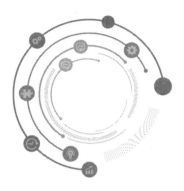

CHAPTER 17

CHANGE AND INNOVATION

by John Horodyski

CHANGE IS EVERYWHERE

Technological innovation results in a constantly evolving business environment that is always changing. Social media is a great example of how technology and communication has created change in our work. Human beings possess an innate desire to interact and socialize, and over the past few decades, new communication technologies—such as email, the Internet, and mobile devices—have become widely adopted. These tools allow us to communicate faster, more frequently, and to a larger audience than previously possible. Social media represents the latest evolution of communication technology, and employees may have a variety of social media technology tools at their disposal. Executives are watching carefully to determine whether corporate social media technology use is merely a passing fad or a process and business technology that will ultimately improve the bottom line or extend a museum's reach.

In another example of present-day change, the Semantic Web allows data to be shared and reused across application, enterprise, and community boundaries. This evolution of the web is changing the existing flow of information within the modern business organization, transforming it into a place where "learning with and from others encourages knowledge transfer and connects people in a way consistent with how we naturally interact." This evolution of the modern business organization may be seen as a fulfillment of the definition of the Semantic Web as a conduit in data sharing, thus transforming business. Information management is central to this change.

Information and all its data and digital assets has become more available, accessible, and in some ways more accountable in business. We live in a big data world, with so much data at our discretion and under considerable watch and scrutiny from our content creators, users, and stakeholders alike. With such change, our organizations need to change also and not only be prepared for the change but respond well and be comfortable with our solutions.

CHANGE MANAGEMENT

Change management is an approach to transitioning or changing people, groups of people, processes, and technology to a desired future state within an organization. The concept and practice of change management was born in the consulting world in the 1980s, driven by the need to understand performance and adoption techniques to allow for greater innovation and organizational adoption methods. One of the premier researchers and thought leaders on change management, John Kotter, reminds us that "70 percent of all major change efforts in an organization fail . . . because organizations often do not take the holistic approach required to see the change through." Change management is a structured approach in an organization to ensure that changes are made in order to achieve some form of long-term benefits. Information management is all about change—changing the way we understand what is an asset, digital and physical, in our organizations and how its value may be transcended throughout all layers of the organization. With such change, the contemporary business organization is motivated by exterior factors (e.g., competition and innovation) to adapt quicker than their competitors so as not to get left behind. Information management is not immune to this dynamic, and as a single source of truth for assets and a digital playground in which to collaborate and create, information management serves a role both as a change agent and as a technology always requiring change within an organization.

In order to effectively manage organizational change, an essential first step is to diagnose the problem and the ability—and more importantly, the capability—to change within your organization. The following best practices are good steps to follow:

1. Recognize the change at a macro level; it's not just a silo or a one-department problem.

2. Develop the change with adjustments for what the organization needs to do.

3. Educate and communicate your organization with the change.

Organizational change management aligns groups' expectations, communicates, integrates teams, and manages people training. It makes use of performance metrics—such as financial results, operational efficiency, leadership commitment, communication effectiveness, and the perceived need for change—to design appropriate strategies, in order to avoid change failures or resolve troubled change projects.

GOVERNANCE

Governance helps us define and manage the change that is needed within an organization—this provides a framework to ensure that program goals are met both during implementation and for the future. Ultimately, this is the only way to manage change and mitigate risk. Governance can begin with a roadmap and measurement tools to ensure success of implementation during the first iteration and may then grow to become formalized into an operating model for the business. Common elements in this model include the regular "suspects" of a project charter, working committee, and timelines so that governance is an ongoing practice transitioning into an operating model. And beyond the delivery of an effective ROI, active governance delivers innovation and sustained success by building collaborative opportunities and participation from all levels of the organization. The more success you have in getting big names involved in the big decisions, keeping them talking about information management, and making this a regular, operational discussion (not just for project approval or yearly budget reviews), the greater the benefits from information management in your organization will have. The best way to plan for future change is to apply an effective layer of governance to your content.

CHANGE IS THE FUTURE

Data sharing and collaboration will play an important part in this change as business rules and policies are created and/or changed in order to maximize the flow of information within an organization to demonstrate innovation. Practitioners within every organization should step back and investigate what they are doing; the practice of information management needs to be explored in greater detail so as to understand how it is being used with individuals and departments across all lines within the business organization. Information management does help organizations create knowledge, share information, develop communication, build access, and promote cooperation, with an emphasis on relationship building. Information management projects can be used to foster a collaborative culture—and in some instances a competitive culture—in business. Information management presents many ways to interact with information, whether it be text, video, audio, or whatever form of rich media. Robinson's (2010) research suggests that when seeking information at work, people rely on both other people and information repositories (e.g., documents and databases) and spend similar amounts of time consulting each (7.8 percent and 6.4 percent of work time, respectively; 14.2 percent in total). Therefore, information management as a strategy may well be a more effective method in which to discover and use information within a business organization.

INNOVATION—UNDERSTAND WHAT'S MOST IMPORTANT TO CUSTOMERS

The Oxford English Dictionary tells us that to "engage" means there is involvement—whether via interest or attention—with someone. It is a process that requires action. Innovative leaders understand that the purpose of business is to create customer value. The most effective organizations today are collaborative networks focused on involving their customers through data collection, monitoring, and ultimately use. The beginning of your information management process must ask the question, "What is most important to our customers?" Customer/user value is a moving target influenced by many factors both inside and outside the organization.

A focus on innovative data and metadata use can generate many positive impacts from information management. Consider the following examples of what powerful effects a content system with good metadata and workflow management may have on users and the organization as a whole:

- support strategic organizational initiatives

- serve as a resource to gauge changes in customer values

- reduce costs

- generate new revenue opportunities

- provide better brand management

- improve collaboration and streamline creative workflow or competitiveness

- enable marketing agility and operational excellence

INNOVATION PROCESS

Drawing inspiration from Rod Collins's book, *Wiki Management: A Revolutionary New Model for a Rapidly Changing and Collaborative World*, there are five fundamental phases to the innovation and change management process that have a direct impact on how digital assets are understood and managed within an organization.

1. **Understand What's Most Important to Customers**

    Innovative leaders understand that the purpose of a business is to create customer value and that the most effective organizations in a rapidly changing world are collaborative networks focused on delighting their customers. The beginning of your information management process must ask the question, "What's most important to your customers?" Customer/user value is a moving target influenced by many factors, both inside and outside the organization. This initial picture of the values influencing consumer choices and the developments that might reshape future market behavior will collate observations from:

    - stakeholder interviews

    - market analyses

    - customer segmentation data

    - industry trends

    - disruptive developments

    - financial analyses

    - winning value propositions

2. **Aggregate and Leverage Collective Intelligence**

The most effective organizations are those that have the capacity to quickly access and leverage their collective intelligence. An effective method to process the initial picture together with your staff is in a collective intelligence lab, where a microcosm of your organization is gathered to

- collectively process key information,

- work cross-functionally in small groups to think holistically and expansively about new and different ways to achieve better results, and

- engage in innovative large group processes to identify the best solutions and their related requirements.

This work results in an innovation portfolio, a strategic framework for proactively managing the growth of your company in a time of change, whether that be for maintenance, incremental change, platform change, or disruptive change.

3. **Build Shared Understanding by Bringing Everyone Together in Open Conversations**

People are more likely to enthusiastically implement what they create. Fostering co-creation can be achieved with collaboration work-thru and iterative check-in sessions. A collaboration work-thru is a facilitated meeting process that empowers a diverse group of individuals to

- quickly co-create a shared understanding of the key requirements for effective delivery,

- identify the key drivers of timely implementation, and

- assure that everyone in the organization is on the right page at the start of critical strategic initiatives or operational projects.

The iterative check-in is a customized cadence for gathering cross-functional teams and updating the shared understanding as changes occur both inside and outside the organization.

4.   **Focus on the Critical Few Performance Drivers**

Information is power, and an important part of effective change management design is making sure that people have the information they need to deliver extraordinary performance. The essence of this phase is the creation of a simple focused scorecard that serves as

- a powerful frame of reference for everyone to independently gauge progress,

- a communication tool to promote high engagement, and

- a mechanism for aligning the distributed work throughout the organization with what's most important to the success of your business.

5. **Hold People Accountable to Their Peers**

Peer-to-peer networks are far more effective than top-down hierarchies for enabling the level of innovation and collaboration needed to keep pace with a rapidly changing world. In this final phase, you need to create customized peer accountability metrics that

- link individual compensation to collaborative action,

- provide incentives for innovative contributions, and

- reward advancing business interests over individual interests.

CHALLENGES IN MARKETING

I never met a data I didn't like.
—Anonymous

Where is innovation in marketing today? Because changes are happening so rapidly in how we conduct business, data must be found in how we create and distribute content and how our customers interact with that content. Innovation must occur inside and out—that is, it must be included in how we create content, as well as how we look at how our consumers interact with that content. The industry shows us that the following is taking place:

- proliferation of media types and media channels

- globalization and the need to release the product everywhere and in every way

- product life cycles are becoming shorter and shorter; the time to market is a shrinking window

- compliance—content is connected, and a content system must maintain those connections

Never more than now, we live in a connected world, and it is comforting to realize that within marketing operations, a content system can be the core of marketing automation and production. An isolated event or activity is not what enables consumer engagement. The best thing to do when embracing challenges is to start by asking the right questions. For example:

- What are the most effective things marketers do?

- What is not effective and why? What must we start doing better?

- Who does this particular thing really well? What do they do that others do not?

- How do we capture the really effective or efficient ways of getting things done via workflow to operationalize others in the firm or supply chain?

We no longer deal with just two or three different kinds of content. The life cycle of the marketing asset is best understood via metadata and workflow. It is foundational to the marketing strategy. There is no splendid isolation in marketing. It is part of an integrated strategy of creation that includes the user, the content creators, the editors, the distributors, the pipeline, and everyone else who is involved in the life cycle of marketing assets. The overall strategy also includes planning, budgeting, creation, review, approval, distribution, and finally use and reuse. The amount of data to be captured here is staggering but ultimately can be used to garner insight into future strategy.

CONCLUSION

Technological innovation results in a constantly evolving business environment as data sharing transforms the organization. Information management is central to this change. Information and all its data and digital assets have become more available, more accessible, and in some ways more accountable in business. We live in a big data world, with so much data at our discretion and under considerable watch and scrutiny from our content creators, users, and stakeholders alike. With such change, organizations need to change also and not only be prepared for the change but also respond well and be comfortable with the strategy and its solutions.

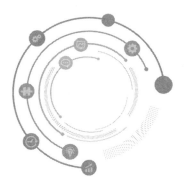

CHAPTER 18

STAKEHOLDER MANAGEMENT

by Chad Beer

WHAT IS STAKEHOLDER MANAGEMENT?

Up to this point, we have discussed various aspects of the management of information and assets that contain it. As information stewards, we must also prioritize how we manage interactions with stakeholders: the people who create, edit, search for, distribute, reuse, or oversee the information and assets. Typically they come from across business units and all along the organizational hierarchy, with widely varied concerns. The interactions include all points of connection that comprise a cooperative partnership, not just top-down directives typically thought of as management.

Practicing meaningful stakeholder management means leading this diverse group of players to:

- embolden them with responsibility, giving them a voice in how information is managed

- establish their collective personal investment and ownership in IM practices

- ensure compliance with established protocol and processes

- embed information management into other responsibilities

Ultimately, stakeholder management aims to ensure that information management activities are collaboratively designed, executed, and continually examined so that processes and technology effectively support stakeholders' responsibilities and the needs of the organization overall. Sounds pretty simple, right?

WHY DOES IT MATTER?

When an information management program is faced with tough challenges (i.e., chronically disorganized assets, lost information, confused stakeholders, etc.), lack of real engagement is often the root cause. As the mechanism by which ongoing, fluid, and collaborative communication occurs between stakeholders and IM managers, stakeholder management is a critical aspect of governance, discussed in chapter 9 of this book. Without it, bad behaviors become habitual and proceed unchecked, potentially without the noncompliant party even being aware they are "breaking rules" or understanding the ramifications.

Let's look at a fictional example. Stakeholder A works at a company that consolidates information to create reports and marketing material for the thriving doughnut industry. Stakeholder A works in the legal department and needs to review assets for copyright concerns. Sadly, A is unsure of where to find them, so she asks a coworker, Stakeholder B. B knows the assets are in a document management system but does not have time to explain how to use the system to A, so he downloads the assets to his desktop and passes them along by email.

After some time, as similar scenarios are repeated over and over and modeled by others, assets are collected and duplicated on multiple desktops and servers, and untracked versions proliferate. Accessing assets from coworkers, users have less and less incentive to learn how to use the document management system. System adoption lags, and over time various stakeholders develop their own workarounds, with no common methodology for organizing or tagging assets. Document versions get lost; approvals or disapprovals cannot be linked to the assets. Unvetted erroneous information is published, and marketing materials use outdated logos and images without proper rights. Worst-case scenario: lawsuits ensue and reputation suffers.

Consistent engagement with stakeholders would address these potential behaviors in several ways, by:

- Training—Delivering recurring sessions about system use and document management processes

- Awareness raising—Educating stakeholders about why it is important to follow prescribed workflows and always use systems of record

- Securing buy-in—Garnering personal investment in the maintenance of IM practices

- Creating feedback loops—Soliciting regular feedback from stakeholders, making opportunities to raise questions, and having discussions about IM practices

- Maintaining oversight—Regularly checking on stakeholder actions, so that out-of-bounds activity, if it occurs, can be noticed and addressed

Consistent engagement allows managers to be aware of misgivings or misunderstandings in the user base that could impact adoption. With a truly collaborative relationship, an information manager can be aware of brewing issues like lingering confusion over system behaviors or employee-created workarounds that point to a need for a revamped process. Such knowledge empowers an IM manager to enact timely changes to continually optimize practices and to stop workarounds before they become embedded socialized habits. Stakeholder management is critical for the wise stewardship that allows an IM program to evolve ahead of problems.

Stakeholder management also allows IM managers to be forward thinking, steering IM practices to address the upcoming needs of the enterprise. Regular conversations with stakeholders create awareness of changes to the business, such as new asset collections that will require integration into IM workflows, new business units and products to be accounted for in a taxonomy, and new use cases that create needs for additional metadata or search terms.

SO IT'S IMPORTANT. SURELY ALL STAKEHOLDERS WILL GET THAT, RIGHT?

As we mentioned, information management practices often touch and rely on the involvement of people from varied teams throughout an organization. Yet as pervasive as IM practices are within an organization, their importance in relation to other tasks can be undervalued or even mysterious to those directly involved with them. Why?

- IM practices are often perceived as add-ons to other, more primary responsibilities.

- The benefits of IM tasks often impact users or activities downstream and so can be perceived as nice to have when faced with competing priorities

- Responsibility over IM practices overall is usually placed exclusively on one dedicated individual or team. Individual stakeholders throughout the information life cycle may not share a sense of ownership and responsibility over IM tasks and will often see it as ultimately the IM manager's problem.

- Organizations frequently fail to provide top-down support for the maintenance of IM practices. Stakeholder A, the fictional legal reviewer mentioned above, may be pressured by management to complete reviews speedily to keep production processes moving, but they are unlikely to be consistently and specifically pressured by upper management to make sure to pull assets only from the system of record. The message relayed to employees is too often "Get it done," not "Get it done correctly."

Concerted effort is required to push through these blocks. The dedication of a range of stakeholders from upper management to data entry teams is required to achieve IM's maximum return on investment. Executive sponsors and upper management must be engaged to maintain their active sponsorship and enforcement. Managers must be engaged to help maintain oversight over IM practices and to relay the importance of their execution to their teams. Those at the lower end of the org chart must be engaged to ensure they understand the relevance and importance of IM tasks.

OKAY, SO IT'S IMPORTANT, BUT WHY DEVOTE A WHOLE CHAPTER TO IT?

Stakeholder management is a frequent recipient of lip service. Even within the information management profession, stakeholder management is rarely given the emphasis it should. Organizations acknowledge the benefits of engagement, outreach, user support, and training. Big changes like the implementation of new technology or the launch of refined processes will often prompt a greater-than-normal degree of stakeholder interaction. Usually, it is not enough. Stakeholder engagement is too often delivered on an as-needed basis. Users and executive sponsors are given trainings when they ask for them, contacted when a problem is identified, reminded now and then through an email to follow specific processes, or occasionally asked for feedback.

Haphazard and lackadaisical engagement only worsens the challenges to prioritizing information management described above. Information management, with its broad reach across an organization, relies on sustained attention and care across and throughout all departments. That sustained attention relies on consistent promotion and enforcement that comes from good management. Managing stakeholders well requires deliberate effort enacted regularly over time as part of the daily business of information management.

PRACTICING STAKEHOLDER MANAGEMENT

How an information manager engages stakeholders depends on the state of an organization's IM practice. Stakeholder management is a critical pursuit during both periods of change and stability. As mentioned above, times of change and transformation will often prompt robust stakeholder interaction, but even when an organization's processes are established and working well, sustained engagement with stakeholders should not be undervalued.

Let's look at what stakeholder management entails for both of these situations.

STAKEHOLDER MANAGEMENT
DURING PERIODS OF CHANGE

CHANGE MANAGEMENT FOR IM PROJECTS, INITIATIVES, AND TRANSFORMATIONS

During major or minor transformations, stakeholder engagement serves many ends.

- allows for all voices to be heard as needs are defined and changes rolled out

- provides hand holding for stakeholders facing potentially stressful changes

- gains buy-in to the changes from all involved

- sets the stage for effective testing and wide adoption

- ensures a positive return on the investment of money, time, and effort to enact the transformation

WHO SHOULD BE INVOLVED AND WHEN

Stakeholder management must be undertaken at all stages of any small or large IM project. Projects often are defined and planned in a vacuum, with a small number of stakeholders having confidently identified a problem and implementing the solution, then looping in others when their opinions or financial backing are needed or the users need to be trained near project completion.

Bringing stakeholders of all levels into the earliest conversations, even during ideation stages, is critical to ensure the projects' success. This applies to relatively small projects like the revision of a metadata model, or large projects like the purchase and implementation of a new enterprise system. If stakeholders in upper management are not engaged from the start, a project may hit a wall once they are asked to provide financial or managerial support. Engaging all players, including end users and data-entry teams, from the beginning ensures that their needs are accounted for and their detailed expertise is utilized.

But which specific stakeholders should be involved in management and engagement activities? In a perfect world, all stakeholders would be directly involved in all levels of engagement. Some degree of consistent in-person collaboration is essential, though many organizations are large enough that ongoing in-person interactions with all stakeholders is just not possible. When this is the case, project managers often establish a project team with stakeholder representatives. It is critical that all levels of organizational hierarchy are represented. Project teams are often composed of many of the same stakeholders that comprise an IM governance council (if established). See chapter 9 for a full discussion of governance.

STAKEHOLDER MANAGEMENT ACTIVITIES

What are the specific actions an information manager should take to establish and maintain stakeholder management during a major project or implementation? Below are some examples:

IDEATION: PROJECT-AWARENESS RAISING

We've discussed how critical it is to make all stakeholders aware of a project from its earliest planning stages. It is most effective to host in-person meetings during which the initiative is described and feedback is solicited from all stakeholders or a designated project team.

ONGOING UPDATES THROUGHOUT THE PROJECT

Once introduced to a project, all stakeholders should receive regular updates about progress and iterative achievements to encourage confidence in the project. Additionally, updates about delays or problems are necessary to keep stakeholders informed and to honor their involvement.

PROJECT REQUIREMENTS DEFINITIONS, SCOPING

The IM manager or project lead must fully understand the needs of everyone affected by the project. For example, if updating a metadata model, one should ensure that all gaps in the current model have been identified so that a single change effort can accommodate all necessary adjustments. Or, if searching for a new technology solution, the project lead should define a thorough requirements list that takes into account the needs of all stakeholders before reaching out to vendors.

VERIFICATION OF PLANNED CHANGES/CONFIGURATIONS

Once needs and requirements are identified and documented, those outputs should be shared with stakeholders for approval. Verification ensures that all needs have been captured accurately and, if needed, gives stakeholders a chance to revise their input. It also allows the project lead to secure stakeholder agreement and document approval before the project can proceed.

ITERATIVE DEVELOPMENT REVIEWS
AND FEEDBACK GATHERING

When possible, a project manager should share changes with key stakeholders as they are being translated from documentation to development and configuration. For example, as a new system is being wire-framed, sharing that iterative development can be tremendously valuable. Previews allow for errors or misunderstandings to be corrected. When translated from documentation to configuration, solutions often look different than imagined and bring to light gaps in planning. Such previews garner excitement by enabling stakeholders to witness their solutions emerge before their eyes and ensures continued sign-off and buy-in as the project proceeds.

TESTING AND FEEDBACK GATHERING

Once completed, any new system or process must be tested. All too often, end user stakeholders are not engaged until this point in a project. When users have been engaged from the outset, they have a full awareness of the purpose of the project and adjustments that have been made during development. This makes for insightful testing that garners truly helpful feedback. These should take the form of hands-on exercises where users actually use the new system or perform the new process, albeit in a development environment.

USER EDUCATION AND ADOPTION

Too frequently, users only become aware of changes to processes or systems when they are brought to a training session. When users have been aware of a project early on and have been able to contribute their input to the needs and requirements, they are likely to greet such trainings with enthusiasm. After the training and subsequent rollout, stakeholders involved from the outset are more likely to abide by the new practices.

Securing stakeholder buy-in from ideation to rollout secures greater compliance and thus less corrective communication down the road. Such an experience also sets a tone of collaborative problem solving. If new needs for change arise in the future, stakeholders are likely to pursue productive avenues for change and avoid workarounds.

STAKEHOLDER MANAGEMENT
DURING PERIODS OF STABILITY

MAINTAINING ESTABLISHED PRACTICES AND RELATIONSHIPS

Stakeholder management remains a critical imperative when an organization's IM practices are at a state of stability. Some mistakenly believe that active engagement with information handlers and system users need only occur when known problems need to be solved. Truly effective stakeholder management requires more than that. It requires consistent and multifaceted interactions.

WHO SHOULD BE INVOLVED AND WHEN

Contrary to periods of change, most stakeholder interactions during stable-state periods should be targeted directly at all users. Stable-state management is an ongoing activity, part and parcel of daily information management. This means that engagement occurs over time, sometimes planned and sometimes opportunistically. Thus, engaging all stakeholders does not mean big presentations to massive audiences. It means that over time, consistently, and when appropriate, engagement will touch all stakeholders, not just team leads or designated representatives.

STAKEHOLDER MANAGEMENT ACTIVITIES

Stakeholder management may occur along a project's life cycle. Below are some examples of specific activities to undertake to establish and maintain valuable ongoing stakeholder management supporting a healthy IM program:

USER FEEDBACK: DIRECT SOLICITATIONS
AND SPEEDY RESPONSES

Stakeholder management is a two-way street. Collaborative relationships underpin every successful information management program. As important as it is that users hear from you (via trainings, etc.), it is just as critical that you hear from them. Without knowing what your stakeholders think, you cannot serve their needs, and so adoption to the processes and systems will fail. During any point of engagement or outreach, user feedback should be clearly requested. Questions, suggestions, and positive feedback are the key to success to an IM manager.

With good feedback comes great responsibility. It is just as necessary to demonstrate that such feedback matters and, when possible, acted on. Users requesting additional training should receive it. Users requesting changes to processes should see such changes being explored, or they should be told why this or that change is not happening. Requests for feedback and input will mean nothing if that input is not acted on or responded to. Users will become dismissive of feedback requests, and the flow of valuable insights will suffer.

TECHNICAL SUPPORT

IM managers are well served to act as the first line of support for users of any IM technology. They are usually super-users of any such system within their organization and are qualified for basic troubleshooting. As needed, of course, issues can be escalated to IT teams or vendors for deeper support. Acting as the bridge between end users and IT teams, information managers hear firsthand about end user issues, develop helpful relationships with users, and promote best practices.

ONGOING TRAININGS

Long after a new system or process is implemented and all users have been trained, it is vital to establish a program of ongoing trainings. Formal trainings in IM practices delivered to new hires not only give information but also set the tone that IM practices are valued by the organization.

Ongoing trainings should also be offered regularly to existing users. Review sessions or deep-dive classes into specific aspects of system behavior keep users engaged, enhance their knowledge, and reinforce best practices for system use.

AUDIT/REPORTING ON BEHAVIOR WITHIN IM SYSTEMS

Many systems provide another very fruitful tool for stakeholder management: tracking and reporting capabilities. With the ability to see how users interact with a system (e.g., what actions they perform, how they search for assets, and which assets are downloaded) an IM manager is able to make sure that best practices are followed; gauge the value and importance of various behaviors, metadata values, and asset collections; and intervene with users when needed.

EXECUTIVE FACING STATUS REPORTS

Recurring status reports are an essential tool for maintaining the support of upper-level stakeholders. After providing financing and endorsement for an IM initiative or program, most executive sponsors expect regular updates about the results of those endeavors. Even if not solicited, they should be provided regularly and presented in person when possible to allow conversations and valuable feedback from those stakeholders.

OUTREACH TO POTENTIAL STAKEHOLDER TEAMS

Finally, an IM manager must direct attention to future and potential stakeholders. Any IM program or system that brings value to the organization stands to bring more value by impacting more teams and users. Reaching out to potential user groups, potentially with system demos or ROI reports, provides a means for bringing more teams and asset collections into the fold, extending the good work of an impactful IM program.

CONCLUSION

Any information management program relies on processes, technology, and people. Without managing stakeholders, IM practices will not succeed. An information manager must be circumspect in their approach to stakeholder management, respecting and accommodating the expertise and concerns of all stakeholders. Leading through consistent collaboration, an information manager will give stakeholders true ownership and investment in the work of IM, and transformative projects and ongoing operations will be designed for success at their inception.

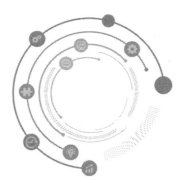

CHAPTER 19

COLLECTIVE INTELLIGENCE

by Rod Collins

What are your organization's most important assets? What is your company's primary means for creating value? What defines the true valuation of your enterprise? If you were to look at your business's financial statements, you might assume it's the value of your plant, property, and equipment. After all, what would happen to your company if, all of a sudden, your physical assets were totally destroyed—vanished and gone forever? How would your organization survive? Would you suddenly be forced out of business? While these might seem like hypothetical questions, they were very real circumstances for one company, which was dramatically confronted by the unthinkable on September 11, 2001.

The corporate headquarters of Empire Blue Cross Blue Shield was located in the north tower of the World Trade Center. While nine of its employees and two consultants lost their lives on that tragic day, over 1,900 workers survived the terrorist attacks. Empire lost over 250 computer servers, over 2,000 desktop computers, and over 480,000 square feet of office space when the north tower collapsed. In a single instant, Empire had lost its headquarters facility and all of its equipment. Yet remarkably, within three days Empire was fully operational. While the company had lost its machines, Empire was fortunate that almost all of its workers survived and its data had been backed up to another site on a regular basis. With its people safe and its data secured, Empire had the essentials it needed to be quickly back in business. Within a matter of hours, the company was able to locate alternative facilities and make the computer hardware arrangements to once again begin processing health insurance claims.

The New York state examiner's report on the recovery efforts of Empire Blue Cross Blue Shield cited three contributing factors in the company's very effective response to the terrorist disaster. First, Empire's disaster recovery plan, especially its regular backup of electronic data, securely preserved the company's critical business information. Second, Empire's continuous quality improvement program created a business environment where all employees understood the operations of the whole company and were aware of how their individual functions impacted other departments and the company as a whole. As a result, despite the catastrophic disruption of their working arrangements, when the employees began reporting to their temporary locations, they understood the specific effects of the disaster and what needed to be done. But perhaps, most importantly, the continuous quality improvement program encouraged employees to act independently and move projects to completion. This proved to be crucial on September 11th between 8:46 a.m., when the first plane crashed into the north tower, and 10:28 a.m., when the tower collapsed.

Despite the chaos and confusion in those first moments after the attack, middle managers at other Empire locations did not hesitate to make critical decisions when they were unable to contact senior management. Their quick thinking and their bold initiative in making important decisions that were usually beyond their normal authority were essential contributions to the data preservation that enabled Empire's resilience.

The important lesson we learn from the Empire story is that, for many twenty-first century businesses, their most critical assets are their data and their people. When yours is essentially a software business, as many—if not most—companies are today, you can literally lose your physical assets and still remain in business. However, if you lose your knowledge assets—your people and your data—you may find yourselves in an unrecoverable situation.

NEW WORLD AND NEW RULES

Since the events of September 11, the technology revolution has accelerated both the capacity and the productivity of knowledge assets. In that time we have witnessed the emergence of Wikipedia and Google as the primary information tools of everyday people as well as the birth of Facebook, Twitter, LinkedIn, and the rest of the social media movement. At the heart of this revolution is the unprecedented networking of the world's people and their data.

We now suddenly find ourselves in a new world with new rules—a hyper-connected world—where, for the first time in human history, mass collaboration is not just possible but highly practical and pervasive. In this short period of time, the fundamental way we structure the world has suddenly shifted from top-down hierarchies to peer-to-peer networks, and in the process we have discovered how to tap into the highest form of human intelligence: our collective intelligence.

Until the Digital Revolution, intelligence was viewed as an individual attribute. Our schools have been designed to develop individuals and pit students against each other in a competition for grades, which explains why most schools consider collaboration to be a form of cheating. Similarly, the typical business organization uses a performance and compensation system designed to recognize and reward individual contributions, assuming that accomplishments can be neatly distributed and ascribed to particular individuals. The traditional organization is built on the assumption that the smartest organizations leverage the intelligence of their smartest individuals. That's why they are designed as top-down hierarchies. The theory assumes, if the smartest people are the ones who rise to the top and we give them the authority to direct and control the work of others, then all the people within the organization will work smarter than they would if left to their own judgments.

But recently, the assumptions behind this theory have been seriously challenged by new technologies that are not only radically rewriting the rules for the way the world works, but more importantly, are creating an unprecedented and incredibly powerful intelligence capacity by providing the practical means for harnessing human collective intelligence. In a post-digital world, the smartest organizations are no longer the ones that leverage the individual intelligence of elite leaders at the top of bureaucratic hierarchies. Rather, they are the ones who have the ability to aggregate and leverage the collective intelligence contained within the full diversity of all the people within their organizational sphere, including sometimes even their customers.

GAME CHANGER

This new reality was dramatically demonstrated in 1998 when two unknown graduate students leveraged the power of collective intelligence to transform the then-young and crowded market of Internet search engines. This market emerged because the web could only become a tool of the masses if people had a way to quickly locate the information they needed from the plethora of data distributed across cyberspace. The original search engine models employed hordes of individual expert editors to rank the importance of web pages. However, none of the many upstart competitors in this new market could establish a dominant position. While many observers at the time expected Yahoo to break out from the pack, a late entrant, Google, using an innovative algorithm that aggregated the wisdom of the crowd, surprised everyone by rapidly capturing two-thirds of the search engine arena, a market position the innovation company has maintained for almost two decades.

With Google, Larry Page and Sergey Brin introduced the world to the first large-scale application of collective intelligence, but more importantly, they convincingly demonstrated the superiority of collaborative peer-to-peer networks over bureaucratic top-down hierarchies as vehicles for producing extraordinary business results. This discovery is game changing because one of the inherent capabilities found in networks and typically absent in hierarchies is the natural tendency to accelerate the flow of both information and ideas, which in turn generates the creation of new information and intelligence.

If knowledge is power, the technology of networks provides a clear competitive advantage to enterprises that know how to aggregate the collective intelligence distributed within their information systems.

MASS COLLABORATION

A few years later, in early 2001, the editors of a fledgling online encyclopedia discovered that, in addition to providing the means for harnessing the collective wisdom hidden in data stocks, the technology revolution was also generating new ways to aggregate the collective intelligence distributed among people. The editors of Nupedia had put a lot of sweat and effort into their quest to build an online encyclopedia. They had assembled a superb group of academic advisors and installed the seven-step hierarchical review process that had been the industry production norm for well over two hundred years. Yet despite their efforts, Nupedia was producing a paltry handful of articles per year. Discouraged, the editors were about to abandon their ambitious project when they seren-dipitously stumbled upon an obscure application popular among software geeks known as a "wiki." Designed by Ward Cunningham, the wiki made it possible for programmers to pool their knowledge and create common staples for the global software community. The visionary encyclopedia editors decided to give their venture one last chance and, despite vehement protests from the academic advisors, embraced the wiki as their fundamental platform, renamed their online venture Wikipedia, solved their productivity problem, and leveraged the power of collective intelligence to radically and dra-matically transform a well-established industry.

Wikipedia introduced an innovative business model made possible by the new mass collaboration technologies of the Digital

Age. Mass collaboration is the capacity for large numbers of geo-graphically dispersed individuals to work directly and effectively with each other without having to go through a central organiza-tion. Instead, they get things done by using the power of networks to aggregate and leverage their collective intelligence to produce extraordinary results.

Mass collaboration is creating entirely new ways of working together that only twenty years ago would have stretched the limits of believability. Who would have imagined that you could build a productive enterprise using only volunteers working without a plan, without assigned tasks, and even without pay? Yet today, Wikipedia is the world's most widely used reference work and has completely displaced a two-century business model in a single decade.

PARADIGM SHIFT

The Digital Revolution has spawned a paradigm shift in the funda-mental architecture for the ways we prospect data and the ways we organize people. The architecture of most information technology systems in the latter half of the twentieth century was hierarchi-cal and reflected the prevailing bureaucratic constructs of the time. Thus, IT systems were mechanically organized into separate files, and the programs used to process information were highly transac-tional and linear. These systems were designed to do work in the way that people would—only far faster and with fewer errors. Where workers had maintained file drawers and worked with those files to produce summary information to guide management decision making, computers mimicked this work process by organizing data into electronic files and compiling reports.

The systems architecture of a post-digital world is very different. Rather than being organized into data files, information resides in a variety of data stocks. In addition to the usual transactional files, these data stocks now include social media, connected devices, software sensors, and other intelligent applications. These nonlinear stocks are organized into highly efficient networks, connecting people and things in revolutionary new ways and achieving levels of extraordinary performance that are often beyond our wildest expectations.

This shift in systems architecture is accompanied by a similar shift in organizational design. For example, when the founders of Google needed to structure their new company as they expanded to keep up with their remarkable growth, they very consciously eschewed the traditional hierarchical model and decided to use the same model that had inspired their search engine. With this in mind, the Google founders built a collaborative network that would leverage the collective knowledge of the many workers distributed throughout the company rather than a top-down hierarchy that would amplify the individual knowledge of the few at the top.

THE WISDOM OF THE CROWD

Technological innovations are expanding the frontiers of human intelligence by turning the rhetorical platitude "nobody is smarter than everybody" into a powerful resource for sustaining extraordinary performance. The newfound capacity to quickly access the collective intelligence resident in both data and people is the defining transformational attribute of our times. Before the Internet, we were substantially limited in our ability to access the collective wisdom of the larger community. Although it has always been true that nobody is smarter than everybody, because we had lacked the technology to organize the intelligence of large numbers of people, access to collective knowledge was simply not practical. Thus, in the days before the web, seeking out the expertise of the brightest among us was the most expeditious course for navigating business success. However, the current state of technology is making it perilous for organizations to endeavor to meet today's market challenges by relying on the judgments of a handful of anointed experts.

James Surowiecki, in his insightful book *The Wisdom of Crowds*, provides numerous examples of where, under the right conditions, groups are highly intelligent and consistently outperform even the smartest individuals in them. In his study of collective intelligence, Surowiecki found that if four conditions are satisfied, groups can provide incredibly sound and accurate judgments.

The first condition is diversity of opinion. Having different perspectives—even eccentric notions—broadens the available information, provides the capacity for evolving ideas, makes it easier for individuals to be candid, and protects against the negative dynamics of shortsighted groupthink.

The second condition is independent thinking, which means that each individual is free to express his or her own opinions without editing and without any pressure to conform to the beliefs of others in the group.

The third condition is local knowledge. In order to truly access collective intelligence, the group must be able to draw on specialized and localized intelligence because the closer a person is to the problem or the customer, the more likely he or she is to have a meaningful contribution. This is why social networks such as the Internet, which include large numbers of people and where no one

245

is in charge, are so valuable; they allow important information to quickly and freely flow from the fringe to the core.

The fourth and final condition is aggregation mechanisms. Without the capacity to collate and integrate the diverse and independent thinking of large numbers of people, there is only chaos and cacophony. Aggregation mechanisms are processes or systems designed to discern the collective intelligence resident in all the various perspectives.

Google and Wikipedia both satisfy Surowiecki's four conditions. Google mines its data by observing the independent and localized choices of the full diversity of users and employing an algorithm mechanism to aggregate the collective intelligence latent in the data. Wikipedia's aggregation mechanism is the wiki, which collates the collective intelligence of the participants by gathering everyone into a common space to effectively integrate the diversity of individual perspectives into one cohesive article.

If, as we learned from Empire Blue Cross Blue Shield, the knowledge streams inherent in a company's data and its people are their most important assets, then competitive advantage in twenty-first century business will belong to those who can best aggregate and leverage the collective intelligence distributed throughout their organizations and within their information systems.

RAPID LEARNING PLATFORMS

The innovative architecture of Wikipedia and Google are examples of how the technological revolution is transforming business through the creation of rapid learning platforms. In addition to web-enabled technologies that transform simple transaction information into valuable collective intelligence, innovative leaders who understand the value of the wisdom of the crowd are embracing learning platforms that allow organizations to reach out to incredibly large numbers of people and to effectively engage all willing participants in collaborative dialogue. Why limit your strategic learning to the knowledge of a handful of executives within your organizational walls when some of the most intelligent people in the world are eager and willing to work with you—sometimes even for free! In a rapidly changing world, the more voices you can get into the same space at the same time, the better the intelligence and the faster you can transform that knowledge into execution—provided that you have workable collective learning processes. Web-based learning platforms are furnishing an unprecedented capacity for organizations to leverage the power of collective intelligence to solve complex problems far faster than they ever imagined possible, as was discovered recently in the health research scientific community.

In the summer of 2011, Firas Khatib, a biochemist at the University of Washington, felt something needed to be done to accelerate the progress of solving a molecular puzzle that had stumped the world's best scientists for more than a decade. The evasive puzzle involved figuring out the detailed molecular structure of a protein-cutting enzyme from an AIDS-like virus found in monkeys. Because this enzyme plays an important role in the spread of the virus, Khatib knew that figuring out its structure could be the breakthrough needed to arrest the medical malady. That's when Khatib turned to Foldit.

Foldit is a collaborative online video game developed by the University of Washington that enlists players worldwide to solve difficult protein-structure problems. There are no special requirements for joining the Foldit community. Everyone is welcome, which explains why most of the more than 235,000 Foldit players have little or no background in biochemistry. Khatib recognized that the molecular challenge was a good fit for the capabilities of the Foldit game. Incredibly, what had evaded the world's best individual scientific experts for ten years was solved by collective knowledge of a diverse group of online gamers within only ten days. When you have the capability to aggregate and leverage collective intelligence within your data and among your people, you discover that there are many times when the wisdom of the crowd does indeed trump the ability of individual experts.

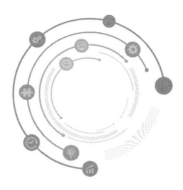

CONCLUSION

by John Horodyski

Content is still "king," and the ability to strategically set the foundation for the kingdom will enable you to take control of your digital assets with good strategy—a digital transformation. However, there are many "thrones" within that deserve and demand your attention in the kingdom. First and foremost, you need to get your digital house in order, know what your internal business units and external partners need, and understand how you will need to deliver assets today—and tomorrow—across multiple channels and devices. The ability to provide content of high value and quality in a timely basis is no longer a wish, as it is the expectation of living in a fast-moving, digital world. And yet, the decision itself to proceed with such a digital transformation enacts a chain of questions to be carefully considered before proceeding. Using strategy, and one based in information management, can effectively deliver knowledge and measurable cost savings, time to market gains, and greater brand voice consistency—valuable and meaningful effects from your content.

Managing information and content is a challenge for most organizations doing business in multiple markets. It is no longer sufficient to have a single policy for content storage, security, retention, and rights management. Each market may have its own set of requirements while also needing to collaborate with others. In addition, the life cycle of digital content may be altered from traditional use cases as new regions are addressed. From inception, there must be an understanding of content use possibilities so that metadata can be designed to support a broad range of use cases. While the ability to leverage content across markets improves its ROI, the risk profile of content increases. To mitigate these risks, quality controls as well as rights management processes must be put in place.

Never more than now, we live in a connected world, and as consistent messaging drives brand loyalty, it is important to define and manage the brand's purpose and function.

1. What are your assets?

2. Where are your assets?

3. What are you trying to do with them?

4. When will you need to access (identify, retrieve, distribute) them?

5. How are you able (rights management) to use them?

As organizations grow in size, evolve and take on additional global market opportunities, change will be the constant for the people, processes, and technology supporting business and marketing operations. Digital transformation plays a critical role in this change, serving as a focused center for digital assets and operations management. Metadata, workflow, technology, and cultural context all affect global operations and must be addressed for many large organizations. Managing global content does not have to be a burden but rather an opportunity to optimize the asset life cycle.

Every strategy needs to start with a foundation—that solid base on which a structure rests and where meaning may be established. There are many structures that deserve attention and preparedness for the roadmap of work to be done in building that foundation. Let the business set the foundation for strategy first and embrace your content, understanding all that you can about what it can do; never stop asking questions. Content requires a foundation for digital strategy. Creating the whole solution—and connecting it throughout your ecosystem—means that your digital assets can be part of this innovation by generating revenue, increasing efficiencies, and enhancing your ability to meet new and emerging market opportunities for your users.

Great content isn't really great until it gets found, consumed, and shared. The opportunity for content owners, marketing technologists, and all those managing content lies in understanding the value of your content and how it can empower their digital operations from creation, to discovery, through distribution. There can be no more reliance or absolute comfort on what was but only the willingness and ability to recognize that change is happening and to become an active participant in that change. For without such action, the risk on brand displacement, loss of intellectual property value, and the fiduciary irresponsibility of not knowing what assets you have will only make it worse to move forward. So, go embrace the change and transform . . . your future depends on it.

CONTRIBUTOR BIOS

(in alphabetical order)

CHAD BEER

Chad Beer has worked with information, content, and asset management for fifteen years, in a range of business environments including publishing, fashion, pharmaceutical advertising, and museums. His career has centered on the development and delivery of operational transformations fueling content strategies. His work has focused on metadata and taxonomy development, rights management, needs assessments, workflow development, system implementation, process change management, and user adoption.

HOLLY BOERNER

Holly Boerner is a senior manager with Optimity Advisors, with fifteen years of experience in the field of information management, particularly in scoping, implementing, and managing business strategies and technology solutions to meet information and content management needs within enterprise environments. She has extensive experience working in consumer packaged goods (CPG), publishing, fashion retail, and advertising industries. She is an active member of the digital asset management (DAM) community and has been a frequent speaker at industry conferences and contributing author to industry journals.

MEREDITH BROWN

Meredith Brown is an experienced associate with Optimity Advisors. She has worked on information management, media and entertainment, and healthcare clients, focusing primarily on change management and increasing businesses efficiencies.

MINDY CARNER

Mindy Carner hails from a small desert town in California where she grew up on a goat farm. She received her bachelor of arts in classical literature from the University of California at Santa Cruz in 2007, and her masters in library and information science from the Pratt Institute in New York in 2011. Mindy's passions for the relics of the past and parallel interest in technological advances led her down an interesting path that combines history (archival theory) with progress (digital media and taxonomic organization).

JESSE CELSO

As a manager with Optimity Advisors, Jesse has extensive experience managing complex engagements for a variety of global media clients. His work has focused on digital asset management, technology implementation, workflow and operational process efficiency, metadata and taxonomy, IP and master data management, rights management, and media content supply chain optimization.

JEREMY COLLINS

Jeremy Collins has a background in mathematics and has been working in software development and consultancy for twenty years. His interest was sparked by logging into a primitive, text-only Internet session in 1992, and since then he has worked with a wide variety of technologies and industries to build solutions that enable users to make the most of their data. Security and data protection has been a strong theme in his work over the last decade.

ROD COLLINS

Rod Collins is the director of innovation at Optimity Advisors. He is a leading expert on management innovation and the author of *Wiki Management: A Revolutionary New Model for a Rapidly Changing and Collaborative World.*

GARETH HARPER

Gareth Harper, PhD, is an experienced economist and data analyst. After completing a masters degree in public policy and a PhD in economics, he had a successful career as an economist working for the UK government, advising on the return on investment of policies in areas as diverse as criminal policy, social security, and correctional services policy. Since joining Optimity Advisors as the chief economist in 2014, Gareth has led teams in providing economic analysis, in particular applying ROI techniques, to a range of business sectors, including developments in the management of digital content.

DAN HAVAS

Dan Havas is a senior associate with over eight years of experience in information management, insurance, and media. He specializes in analyzing metadata and workflows, as well as project management.

VERONICA HSIEH

Veronica Hsieh is an associate at Optimity Advisors who has worked with clients in a range of industries including consumer products, media and entertainment, insurance, and financial services. Her experience has been focused around improving business processes such as streamlining operations and reporting

ROBERT MOSS

Robert Moss is one of the leaders of Optimity Advisor's technology advisory practice. An experienced technology and strategy leader, he helps organizations understand and adapt to the new technologies that are disrupting traditional business models as well as design and build high-performing enterprise applications. Robert works with clients in a range of industries, including health care, media and entertainment, and insurance and supports them as they formulate and execute key technology initiatives such as online commerce, web and mobile application development, and advanced data management.

GRETCHEN NADASKY

Gretchen Nadasky is a manager at Optimity Advisors who leads records management projects for large international clients. Gretchen initiates enterprise records programs and governance strategies including corporate records policies, retention schedule construction, and change management. She is known for success guiding clients to make informed decisions about records, transform operations, and outperform efficiency goals.

REID ROUSSEAU

Reid is a senior associate with Optimity Advisors and has worked collaboratively on digital transformation projects across industries including media and entertainment, consumer packaged goods, and health care. Reid loves the challenge of guiding organizations through the strategic, operational, and technology decisions required in the age of digitization. His experience includes technology selection and implementation, digital asset management strategy, and metadata and taxonomy design.

MADI SOLOMON

Madi is a senior manager and is a creative technologist who specializes in business intelligence initiatives and semantic technologies that bridge the technical with social and cultural constructs. She has held executive roles in large multinational companies and has initiated and led business transformation programs from the ground up.

NICK THORPE

Nick Thorpe is an associate with Optimity Advisors, who has worked with clients in industries such as aerospace, online retail, media and entertainment, and healthcare. He has experience in process improvement, financial reporting, compliance, data migration, and cloud computing.

RORY TIERNEY

Rory Tierney is a senior economist at Optimity Advisors, experienced in designing and conducting return on investment and cost-benefit analysis. He has worked for both private and public clients in health care, criminal justice, and financial services and presented research at conferences held by the Society for Benefit-Cost Analysis and the American Society for Criminology, among others.